HOW TO *write* AN ADMISSION WINNING SOP

THE POWER OF STORYTELLING

NIMISHA PADLIYA

In loving memory of...

Papa, you are my constant source of inspiration and guiding light. Although you are not with us, your presence continues to be felt in my heart and in every aspect of my life. Your memories, teachings, and principles have shaped the person I am today and continue to illuminate my path.

Going against the tide, you made the bold decision to send me overseas for graduate studies and build my future. Everything I have accomplished today is a result of your sacrifices and firm convictions. My success is a testament to your faith in me and my capabilities. You celebrated my smallest of achievements with utmost joy, and your pride in my accomplishments remains a driving force.

This book is dedicated to you, Papa, as your love and support continue to inspire me. Thank you for blessing my life with your wisdom and strength.

With eternal love and gratitude,

Nimisha

Contents

BONUS CHAPTERS

ACKNOWLEDGMENT

I would like to express my heartfelt appreciation and gratitude to the following individuals who have been instrumental in my writing journey.

To the two most important men in my life – my husband and my son – thank you for all those midnight coffee brewings and for dealing with my writer's block tantrums. Your understanding, patience, and support when I needed to focus on my book have been remarkable.

To my beloved Mother, my first teacher, my compass, thank you for always steering me in the right direction. You have consistently emphasized the importance of education and encouraged me to pursue my dreams.

To Scholarly and all my mentors, thank you for your guidance and expertise. Your knowledge and insights have shaped my perspective and inspired me to strive for excellence.

To my students, who motivated me to pen down this book, I am deeply grateful for your support and willingness to share excerpts from your essays for inclusion in the book (anonymously), which will undoubtedly benefit aspiring applicants. Your contribution is sincerely acknowledged.

PREFACE

Congratulations! You are holding this book, which means you (or your loved ones) are willing to study abroad and do not want to leave any stone unturned in securing admission to your dream university. I truly appreciate you taking the time and effort to read this book in this digital age, where information (or misinformation or disinformation) – customized, personalized, and organized – is at your fingertips.

The main source of motivation behind writing this book is the amazing feedback I have received from students over the past 10 years of my experience in overseas education.

There are five pivotal components of a university application:

1. Academic Performance
2. Standardized Test Scores
3. Extracurricular Activities & Community Service
4. Letters of Recommendation
5. Statement of Purpose

The scope of this book is the last component, that is, the Statement of Purpose.

While it is true that we do not have the ability to go back in time and alter our grades, academic performance, and/or achievements (though many of us wish we could!), what we do possess is the superpower to shape our future, our destiny by writing a compelling statement of purpose and gaining admission to our dream university. However, as Winston Churchill rightly said, *"Where there is great power, there is great responsibility,"* it is essential to acknowledge the responsibility of starting early and dedicating ample time to the Statement of Purpose component of our application.

At the time of application, students get bombarded with the requirement of a barrage of documents like transcripts, letters of recommendation, financial documents, standardized test scores, resume, rank certificate, bank statements, and so on. In such turmoil, a statement of purpose often takes the backseat until the deadline appears at point-blank range. Making last-minute changes and revisions can be detrimental, leaving the statement of purpose in a disarrayed state. Needless to say, no one enjoys reading such poorly structured and disorganized essays.

To avoid this situation, it is best to begin early, ideally six months in advance, to steer clear of any last-minute chaos and ensure a well-written essay.

How to Write an Admission Winning SOP is an invaluable companion for students aspiring to pursue higher education overseas. With real-life examples, SOP excerpts, and step-by-step guidance, this book isn't just a guide; it's a journey you embark on with your dreams as the destination. Unlike other books, it encourages hands-on learning.

Don't leave your future to chance. Empower yourself with the knowledge, examples, and skills you need to make your SOP truly outstanding. Whether you're a high school student aspiring to study abroad or a graduate applicant looking to advance your career, this **DIY SOP writing book** is your key to unlocking the doors of your dream university.

HOW TO USE THIS BOOK?

In today's fiercely competitive landscape of international admissions, your Statement of Purpose (SOP) serves as your beacon of hope, your voice, and your ticket to your dream university. This book can be your personal roadmap to crafting compelling SOPs that can tilt the admission-decision scales in your favor.

After interviewing several students and parents about the SOP writing process, I realized that there are three main reasons for procrastinating:

1. Hesitation to pen down your thoughts
2. Skeptical about where and how to begin
3. Fear of getting the grammar, sentence structure, or story wrong

To help you break this barrier and come out of your cocoon, I have designed this user-friendly, DIY book to assist you in scribbling your ideas without interrupting the chain of thoughts, and most importantly, thinking out loud without any hesitation, skepticism, or fear!

This book has numerous examples and samples demonstrating various pieces of a Statement of Purpose. As you progress through its pages, you'll find interactive exercises and templates that will allow you to apply what you've learned in real-time, write your own pieces, and refine your SOP on the go.

Rest assured, by the time you finish reading this book, you will be done writing the first draft of your statement of purpose.

It is pertinent to emphasize that various samples, examples, and excerpts in the book are for demonstration and understanding purposes only and any form of replication is totally discouraged. Needless to say, your Statement of Purpose must be original and your compilation alone.

The Universities, Colleges, Schools, and organizations mentioned in the book are for illustration purposes only; I have no affiliation with these institutions.

Nevertheless, *How to Write an Admission Winning SOP* is your ultimate SOP companion, your mentor, and your passport to academic success. Start your journey today, and let your SOP speak volumes about the exceptional student you are.

Early Bird Reward

For the first 10 students who will share their draft along with snapshots of the book's interior adorned with notes and markings, I will assist them in proofreading their academic Statement of Purpose. Scan the QR code to connect with me.

1

WHAT IS A STATEMENT OF PURPOSE (SOP)?

A Statement of Purpose, commonly known as SOP, is a written document that students are usually required to submit along with other documents when applying for an undergraduate, graduate, or research program, mainly to US, Canadian, UK, Australian, Singaporean, or European universities.

It is believed that Harvard was the first University to include SOP as a part of its application process. Other US universities followed suit, and now SOP has become a standard requirement for most graduate programs in the United States.

Over the years, the format and content of the SOP have evolved, and it is now used by universities worldwide to evaluate candidates for admission to graduate and research programs.

The purpose of an SOP is to present the Admission Officer with your:

- Academic Upbringing
- Professional Background
- Career Aspirations
- Extracurricular Achievements
- Suitability for the program and
- Dedication and drive to pursue your area of study

Depending on the geography you are applying for, **SOP can also be termed as**:

- Personal Statement or Personal Essay
- Letter of Intent
- Statement of Interest
- Motivation Letter
- Research Statement
- Academic Essay
- Academic Statement & Personal History Statement

These may differ in the format (word limit, page length, font size, character count, etc.); however, content-wise, all these essays require students to highlight their - unique background, qualities, and experiences; emphasize their research interests and academic accomplishments; and elaborate on how the program will help them achieve their career goals.

2

IMPORTANCE OF SOP

Think of SOP like a navigation system in a vehicle. It provides a route (the applicant's journey) and real-time feedback (motivations and goals) to reach the desired destination (academic program).

Let's better understand the importance of SOP using a Navigation System analogy:

★ **Setting the Destination:** You start by entering your destination address. Admission Officers are looking for students with a vision or a dream they are passionate about. SOP is the right place to talk about your future goals and career aspirations.

> **Example:** *While pursuing PhD in Behavioral Psychology is my primary goal upon completing the MSc in Psychology program, my long-term objective is to work as a Professor in*

an academic setting where I can impart knowledge to others as well as conduct research in my field of interest. And I am certain that my zeal for challenges combined with cutting-edge research at University College London would enable me to translate my aspirations into reality.

★ **Calculating the best route to reach your destination:** Outline the path you've taken so far in your academic or professional life in the SOP. Research Work, Online Courses, Summer Internships and Passion Projects are some examples of ways to demonstrate your subject knowledge beyond the textbook and ability to succeed at the University.

> **Example:** *As a final year B.Tech student, Mechanical Engineering, I was exhilarated when I was selected for the most coveted summer internship in agriculture automation at UIUC wherein I would tackle a real-world problem. Having previously worked on AI powered tractors, smart irrigation systems, and farming robots, I was deeply fascinated by the groundbreaking work of eminent professors at the Grainger College of Engineering, which aimed at identifying the positive and negative obstacles in agriculture. Over the course of two months, I conducted field tests of my algorithm in Illinois Apple Orchards, and the outcomes of*

my research were subsequently published in an international journal.

★ **Encountering roadblocks, detours, or diversions from a direct course:** SOP is the perfect place to talk about the challenges you overcame to arrive at this stage in your life and/or the difficulties you faced while accomplishing your goals. This may include any educational barrier, physical disability, financial hardship or mental stress to name a few.

> **Example:** *My journey has been one of resilience and transformation, as I faced the challenges of body-shaming and weight issues due to PCOD syndrome. Instead of succumbing to adversity, I fought back with grit and willpower. Through consistent workouts and a balanced diet, I have not only qualified for the TCS New York Marathon but have also become an inspiration to 37 other girls struggling with obesity. Over the last four years, I've guided them on a path to fitness through sports and proper nutrition. Now, I aspire to further my passion by pursuing a Master of Science Degree in Sports Science at Texas A&M, where I can continue my journey of empowerment and make a lasting impact in the field of sports and wellness.*

★ **Real-time guidance**: While driving, navigation system provides real-time assistance, such as "Turn left in 500 meters." In an SOP, motivations are like these real-time cues. By incorporating such motivations from your life in a thoughtful and strategic way, you can make a compelling case for why you are the right candidate for the program or institution you are applying to.

Example: *I hail from the stunning Maldives, a place known for its breathtaking blue lagoons and picturesque white beaches. It may seem like an ideal paradise for tourists, but as a student, I've encountered some profound challenges at the grassroot level. These challenges include geographical isolation and a lack of access to essential resources like computers, the internet, and even textbooks. These glaring disparities have posed formidable hurdles on my educational path. However, with wholehearted support from my parents, who firmly believe in breaking the shackles of poverty through literacy, I managed to rise above these obstacles and pursue a bachelor's degree in sociology.*

Now, fueled by an ardent desire to make a meaningful contribution to my community, I am determined to advance my education through a Master's program in Community Development at Monash University. My ultimate aspiration is to empower my Maldivian community, especially children, to overcome similar obstacles and realize their aspirations, thereby nurturing a brighter future for our beloved nation.

★ **Measuring progress while ensuring focus:** Just like a navigation system estimates your time of arrival and keeps you on the right track, your SOP should also provide a timeline of your academic journey, highlighting key milestones, without digressing from the actual goal.

> **Example:** *During final year of my B.Arch degree, I experienced a devastating car accident that left me with a fractured right arm. This unfortunate event prevented me from taking my university exams, leading to a gap year in 2019. As someone who had been honored with the 'Dean's Award' for four consecutive years, this setback was truly disheartening. To make matters worse, the Covid pandemic extended my college break by another two years. Initially, I felt lost and stuck. However, it was during these challenging times that the YouTube Channel 'XYZ Architect' became my lifeline. I became deeply captivated by these educational videos, which inspired me to start my own social media channel – AnokheNazaare – to share my architectural knowledge with the world. Remarkably, within just one month, I had amassed 500 subscribers, and today, I proudly hold the YouTube Silver Play button as a testament to my dedication. Recognizing my*

passion for teaching and my knack to explain complex concepts with ease, my professor extended an offer for a teaching assistant position upon my return in 2022.

★ **Arriving at your destination with confidence:** When you reach your destination, you do so with confidence. In the concluding paragraph of the SOP, you must give the reader a clear sense of who you are and what you bring to the table with the assurance that you are well prepared and determined to succeed.

> **Example:** *Opting for Biotechnology as my major was an unexpected twist of fate. Initially, I had my heart set on pursuing a career in medicine, a perfect match to marry my keen interest in biology with my desire to make a meaningful impact on humankind, and had even secured admission to a prestigious medical college, 1000 km away from home. However, fate threw me a curveball when I was diagnosed with type-1 diabetes, and as a precautionary measure, my parents decided to enroll me in a college close to home. Surprisingly, this redirection has guided me onto a path that resonates deeply with my calling and passion. When I reflect on the journey I've embarked upon, it feels like a thrilling adventure, reinforcing the wisdom of Master Oogway, "One often meets his destiny on the road he takes to avoid it."*

In summary, consider SOP as an ideal platform to substantiate your goals, relevant qualifications, motivations, and a well-defined path towards your academic or career destination, one that provides the reader with a clear and purpose-driven narrative.

3

SOP Fundamentals

Before we begin writing the SOP, answer these five fundamental questions:

1. How do your academic background and career objectives correlate to your aspiration to pursue higher education?

The Admission Officers aim to assess your commitment level towards your intended academic and professional areas of interest by examining the coherence and relevance of your essays/SOP. Therefore, the essay should present a well-connected and cohesive narrative to showcase your focus and dedication.

Points to ponder: *Projects and research work done at school and/or college level; participation in co-curricular activities ranging from workshops and conferences to competitions and student clubs;*

internships or professional experience gained under some professor or industrial expert; independent projects and research paper publication; online coursework; mentoring/tutoring other students, etc.

____

____

____

____

____

____

____

____

____

____

____

____

2. What has inspired you to pursue a graduate degree in your field of interest?

Highlight your accomplishments, demonstrate your enthusiasm, and exhibit your expertise through real-life examples and anecdotes if you have been working in the same field for an extended duration.

Points to ponder: *Recognition received at the workplace; client/customer appreciation; skills and knowledge gathered along the way; achievements that are quantifiable through numbers, data, success stories, or promotions.*

____

____

____

____

____

____

____

____

____

____

____

____

However, if you intend to transition to a different field of interest, you must convince the Admission Committee about your plans and domain knowledge. SOP is the best place to persuade the university and show that you have thoroughly evaluated your decision and possess the potential to thrive and excel in the new area.

Points to ponder: *Extra coursework or subjects taken to enhance your understanding of the field; any professional experience or projects that illustrate your zeal for challenges; activities that showcase your multi-talented personality.*

____

____

____

____

____

____

____

____

____

____

____

____

____

3. How will you contribute to the student community at your future university?

Top universities are looking for leaders, visionaries, and changemakers – those who can drive a positive change in their community and environment while at the university and even thereafter. As a student, you should be willing to participate in extracurricular activities on campus and contribute to student diversity.

Points to ponder: *Participation in extracurricular activities like sports, music, art, debates, public speaking, cultural events, technical festivals, editorial boards; leadership roles; volunteer initiatives; community service; outreach programs; positions of responsibility.*

____

____

____

____

____

____

____

____

____

____

____

____

4. What role will a graduate degree play in your career advancement?

At this stage, you are expected to possess a certain level of independent thinking and should have a clear idea of why you want to study further. Why do you want to study further at this stage of your career? What is the motivation behind pursuing a graduate degree? Clearly define your short-term and long-term goals and explain how a graduate degree fits within those specifications and expectations.

Points to ponder: *Better career prospects; excellent research opportunities; world-class academic facilities; recommendations from friends, family, or alumni.*

____

____

____

____

____

____

____

____

____

____

____

5. Why do you want to pursue a graduate degree from a particular school/university?

Are you looking for scholarship? Is there a particular Professor you want to work with? Or is it because alumni speak highly of this school? Irrespective of the reason, research the university website thoroughly to ensure that the university's vision and mission are in synergy with your career plans and academic objectives.

Points to ponder: *Subjects and electives being offered at the university; Professor names and research areas; projects you would like to work on; student clubs and organizations; career prospects; diversity of students; on-campus placements; career fairs; student - teacher ratio; location of the campus; overall tuition and living expenses; scholarships/assistantships offered.*

4

SOP WRITING PROCESS

The process of writing a Statement of Purpose typically involves five steps, each vital for crafting a captivating and effective essay. The steps are:

1. Introspect
2. Write
3. Analyze
4. Research
5. Edit

SOP WRITING STEPS

Figure 4.1: SOP Writing Steps

Let's delve into each step:

1. **Introspect**: *"Know thyself."* This famous quote by the Greek philosopher Socrates, emphasizes the significance of self-reflection. Self-reflection helps us to gain a deeper understanding of ourselves, our values, strengths, weaknesses, and desires, enabling us to tell an honest, straight-from-the-heart story aligned with our true selves.

   To help you navigate through the introspection process, I have discussed some unique brainstorming techniques in Chapter 5.

2. **Write**: The writing stage involves putting your thoughts and ideas into words. Start by crafting a strong opening that grabs the reader's attention, then

develop each section with clarity and precision. Provide relevant examples, experiences, and achievements that support your claims and demonstrate your qualifications. Strive for a concise and engaging writing style while maintaining a professional and formal tone. Ensure that your ideas flow smoothly and that the content aligns with the intended message.

In Chapters 6, 7, and 8, you will identify the appropriate flow for your SOP, learn how to create a blueprint, and ultimately, integrate all the components together in well-organized paragraphs.

3. **Analyze**: The next step is to analyze the SOP prompt, that is, thoroughly understand the requirements and expectations outlined in the University SOP prompt. It involves perusing, parsing, and interpreting the instructions, identifying key themes or questions, and grasping the purpose and audience of the SOP.

   In chapter 9, titled *Parsing the Prompt*, you will enjoy the exercise of analyzing several different university SOP prompts.

4. **Research**: Once the prompt is clear, it's essential to conduct a thorough university research. This stage involves gathering information about the academic institution, program, or field of study to which you are applying, as highlighted in Chapter 10. It may also include exploring relevant industry trends, current issues, or academic advancements. Research helps you

align your goals, experiences, and aspirations with the program's objectives.

5. **Edit**: Editing is the final stage of the SOP writing process and imperative for refining your document. Review your SOP to ensure it is free of grammatical errors, spelling mistakes, punctuation issues, and maintains clarity. Consider seeking feedback from experts, such as mentors or counselors, to gain different perspectives. Chapter 11 provides a detailed list of common mistakes to steer clear of or remove any inadvertent creep-ins and churn out an outstanding write-up.

By following this five-step SOP writing process, you can effectively convey your experiences, goals, and qualifications in a well-structured and impactful manner. Remember to allocate sufficient time for each stage to ensure a polished and compelling Statement of Purpose.

5

INTROSPECTION

Introspection is a pivotal step that involves brainstorming your thoughts, ideas, and key points. It includes outlining the preliminary structure of your SOP, deciding on the main themes or arguments you want to convey, and creating a logical flow for your content.

Brainstorming Techniques

"Rome wasn't built in a day."
~ John Heywood

Similar is the case with SOP writing. You cannot, or must I say, '*should not*' attempt to write it on the last day of your application deadline. Rather, it is a long-drawn, well-thought-out process; one that requires serious contemplation and brainstorming.

In this chapter, I will discuss four super effective techniques for visualizing and conceptualizing your thoughts, stories, and flow together.

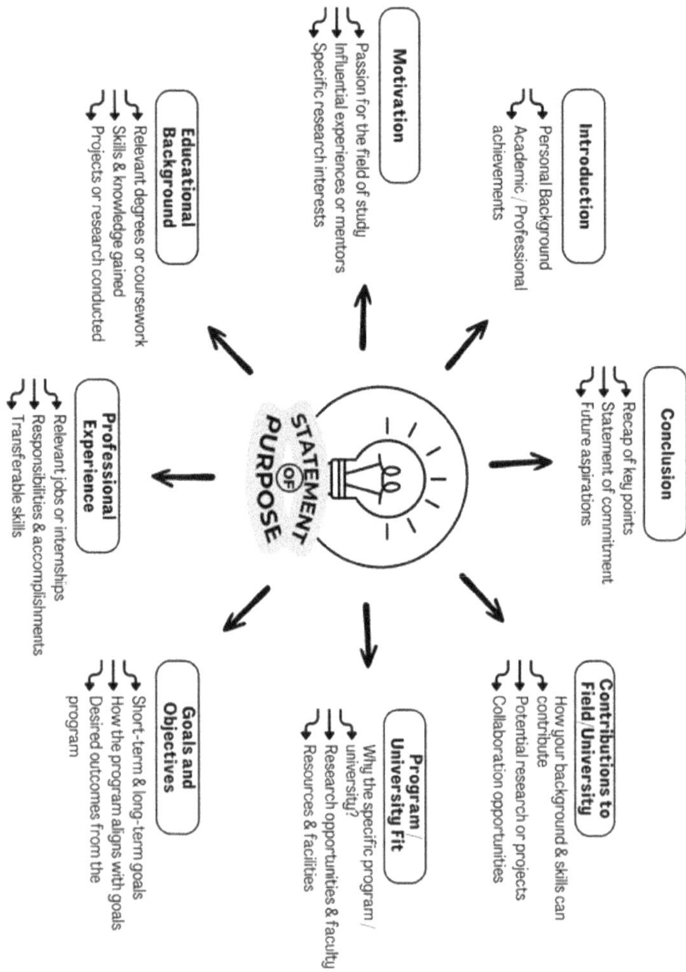

Figure 5.1: Mind Map Schema

1. Mind Map

The Mind Mapping technique can be a valuable tool for organizing and brainstorming your thoughts while writing an SOP.

Follow these steps to effectively use the Mind Mapping technique:

a. **Start with the main idea**: Begin by placing the main idea or topic of your SOP in the center of a blank sheet of paper. This could be your overarching goal, motivation, or the purpose of your application.

b. **Branch out with key themes**: From the center, create branches radiating outward, representing the main themes or sections you want to address in your SOP. These themes could include academic achievements, research experience, career goals, personal qualities, or any other relevant aspects.

c. **Generate sub-ideas**: For each theme, generate sub-ideas or sub-topics that are related to it. Write these sub-ideas as branches stemming from their respective themes. These sub-ideas can be specific accomplishments, experiences, skills, or characteristics that support the main theme.

d. **Expand with details and examples**: Further expand each sub-idea by adding more branches or sub-branches. Include specific details, examples, anecdotes, or evidence to support and illustrate your points. This will help you provide depth and specificity to your SOP.

e. Make connections: Look for connections and relationships between different branches. Identify overlapping ideas, complementary experiences, or recurring themes. This will help you create a cohesive narrative.

f. Prioritize and structure: Assess the importance and relevance of each branch and sub-branch. Prioritize the most significant points that align closely with your purpose and the requirements of the program. Arrange the branches in a logical order that creates a clear and coherent flow.

g. Transfer to writing: Once you have completed the Mind Map and have a clear structure, use it as a guide to start writing your SOP. Begin with the main idea and address each theme and sub-idea systematically, expanding upon the details and examples you brainstormed.

The Mind Mapping technique allows you to visually organize your thoughts, make connections between ideas, and create a logical structure for your SOP. It encourages creativity, flexibility, and a holistic approach to brainstorming and organizing your ideas effectively.

2. Freewriting Technique

The Freewriting technique, as illustrated in *Figure 5.2* allows you to tap into your subconscious and unleash your creativity, enabling a free flow of ideas and thoughts.

Follow these steps to effectively use the Freewriting technique:

a. **Set a time limit**: Allocate a specific amount of time for your freewriting session. It can be anywhere between 10 and 20 minutes, depending on your preference and availability.

b. **Start writing non-stop**: Begin writing without any inhibitions or concerns about grammar, punctuation, or coherence. Write continuously, allowing your thoughts to flow naturally. Do not worry about structure or organization at this stage. For this technique to work, it is imperative that you write on paper as against typing a document to preempt the temptation of editing the write-up midway.

c. **Focus on the main topic**: Keep your SOP's main topic or purpose in mind as you write. Concentrate on expressing your motivations, experiences, goals, and qualifications related to the program or field of study you are applying to.

> *Why should I pursue a career in a particular field? I want to pursue a career in finance...because...it encompasses my passion for numbers, problem solving, analytical, strategic thinking. The world of finance fascinates me with its intricate web of markets, investments, and financial systems. It offers the opportunity to analyze data, identify patterns, and make informed decisions that can have a ~~deep~~ profound impact on ~~business~~ businesses and individuals. Finance also presents a dynamic and ever-evolving landscape, which appeals to my desire for constant learning and ~~constant~~ growth. I am drawn to the challenge of navigating through uncertainties/evaluating risks/creating value. Provide latest news examples like Russia-Ukraine War, Covid-19 Pandemic, Demonetization etc. A career in finance aligns with my strengths and interests and passion, providing a platform to contribute to the success and stability of MNCs while continuously expanding my knowledge and skills.*

Figure 5.2: Freewriting Technique

d. Write without self-censorship: Don't hold back or edit yourself while freewriting. Let your thoughts and ideas emerge freely, even if they seem incomplete or fragmented. This technique encourages you to bypass your inner critic and encourages creative and spontaneous thinking.

e. **Embrace tangents and connections**: It is common for new ideas, tangents, or connections to arise during freewriting. Embrace them and allow yourself to explore those thoughts. They may lead to valuable insights or unique perspectives for your SOP.

f. **Review and highlight key points**: After the freewriting session, read through what you have written. Identify key points, experiences, or ideas that stand out as relevant and important for your SOP. Highlight or underline those sections to focus on during the next step.

g. **Organize and structure:** Use the highlighted sections from your freewriting session as the basis for organizing and structuring your SOP. Identify common themes or threads, and group related ideas together. Determine the logical flow and sequence for presenting your thoughts.

Freewriting technique helps you overcome writer's block (discussed in detail in Chapter 11), generate raw material, and discover unique perspectives for your SOP. Use this technique as a starting point and later refine your ideas during the writing stage.

3. Affinity Wall

Building an Affinity Wall using sticky notes is another helpful Brainstorming technique.

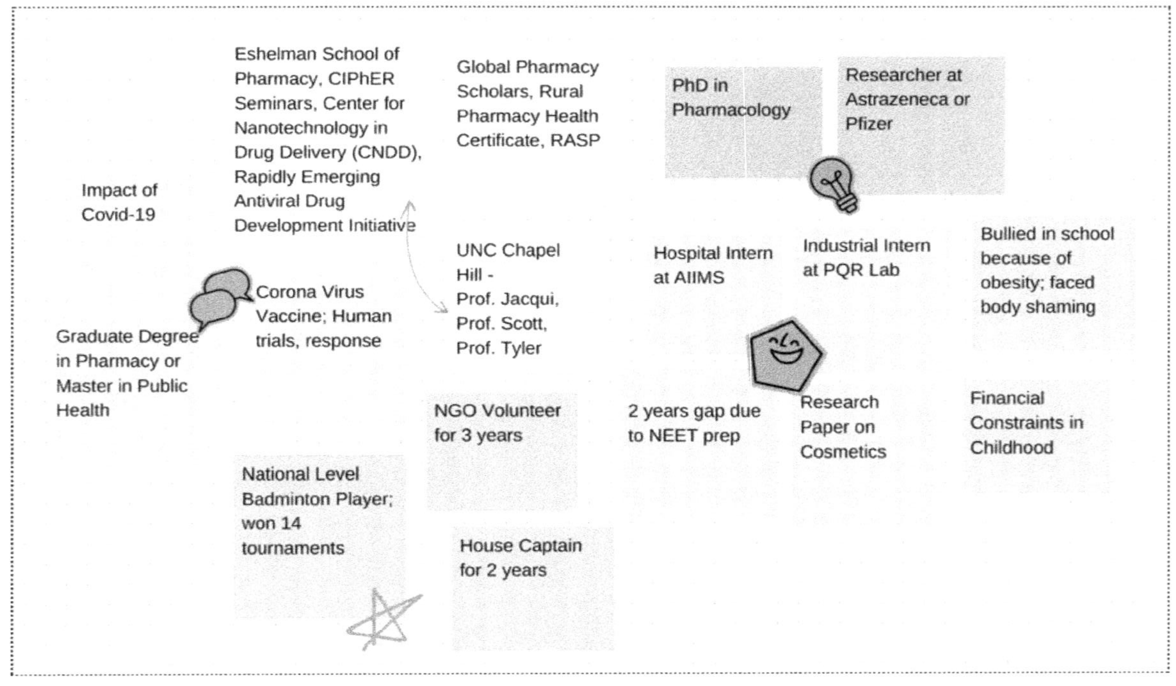

Figure 5.3: Affinity Wall - Scattered

Here's a step-by-step guide to build an Affinity Wall:

a. **Gather materials**: Get a pack of sticky notes in different colors and a large blank wall or board where you can create your Affinity Wall.

b. **Identify key themes**: Start by identifying the main themes or categories that you want to cover in your SOP. These could be your academic achievements, research experience, career goals, personal qualities, or any other relevant aspects. Put each theme/category on an individual sticky note.

c. **Generate ideas**: Take one sticky note at a time and note down specific ideas, examples, or stories related to that theme. Use a different color for each idea or subcategory. Do not worry about organizing them at this stage; focus on generating as many ideas as possible.

d. **Arrange the sticky notes**: Once you have multiple sticky notes with ideas, it's time to organize them on the Affinity Wall. Start by placing the sticky notes randomly on the wall, giving each idea its own space.

e. **Create connections**: Look for commonalities or connections between the sticky notes. Move them around, grouping related ideas together. This process helps you identify patterns, themes, or overarching concepts within your thoughts.

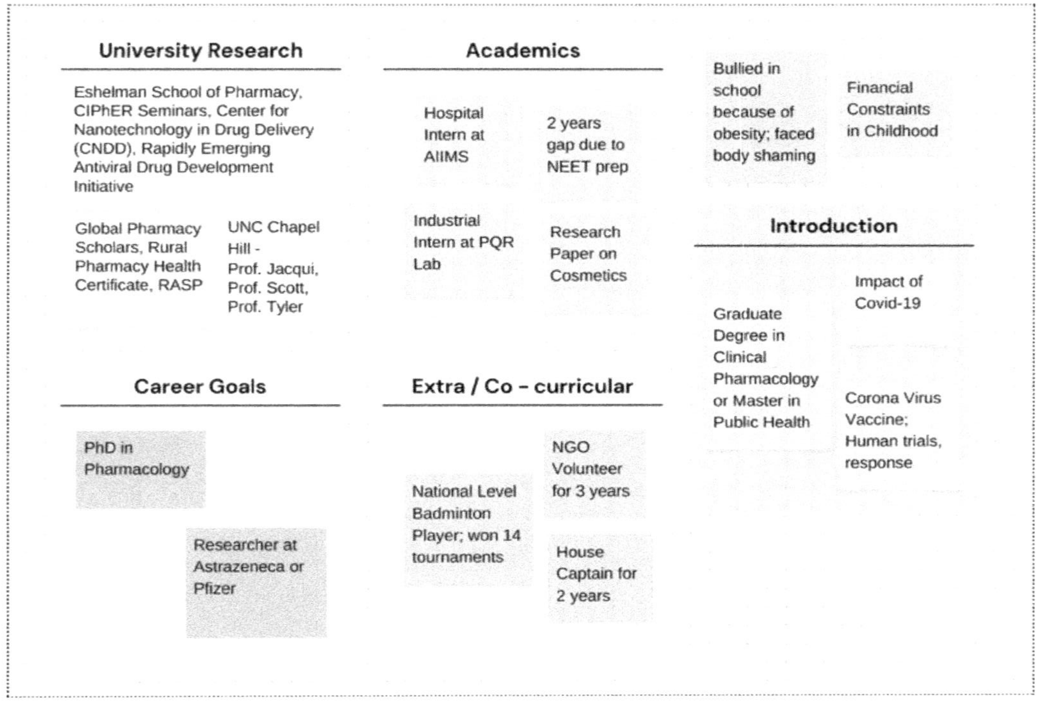

Figure 5.4: Affinity Wall – Structured

f. Establish a structure: Based on the grouped sticky notes, start creating a framework or structure for your SOP. Determine the main sections or paragraphs that will make up your document. Write those section headings on additional sticky notes and place them accordingly on the Affinity Wall.

g. **Refine and finalize**: Once you have a clear structure, review the content of each sticky note within its respective section. Assess the lucidity and flow of ideas. Rearrange sticky notes as needed to improve the logical progression of your thoughts.

h. **Transfer to writing:** With the organized structure and refined content in place, begin writing your SOP based on the sticky notes. Expand upon each idea, providing more context, elaboration, and supporting evidence.

Similar to Mind Maps, the Affinity Wall is also a powerful visual aid for efficient organization of thoughts. It can be modified, expanded, or rearranged as you progress in your writing process. The ultimate goal is to develop a well-structured and cohesive SOP that showcases your qualifications, experiences, and goals clearly.

4. **Cornell Notes** [v]

The Cornell Notes is a functional note-taking method for systematically organizing and summarizing your ideas. It can be effectively customized to provide a structured framework for writing your SOP.

TOPIC

Cue / Questions

- What sparked my passion for computer science?

- How have my experiences influenced my interest?

- What specific projects or research have I undertaken?

- What are my future aspirations and goals?

- Why is the program/university a good fit for me?

Main Ideas

- Why am I interested in the program/field?
  - Passion for computer science
  - Love for problem-solving through technology
  - High school programming class experience

- Key experiences & projects that shaped my interest
  - Summer internship at tech company
    - Collaborative environment
    - Witnessing the power of technology
  - Developing a mobile app for sustainability
    - Addressing real-world challenges
    - Creativity and innovation

- Academic achievements & relevant coursework
  - Advanced courses in algorithms, data structures, AI
  - Strengthened problem-solving skills
  - Research experience in machine learning

- Future aspirations & career goals
  - Desire to contribute to technological advancements
  - Making a difference in society through innovation

- Fit with the program & university
  - Esteemed computer science program at XYZ University
    - Renowned faculty
    - State-of-the-art facilities
  - Collaborative & diverse community
    - Embracing different perspectives
    - Working together for positive change

- Conclusion
  - Summary of passion, experiences, and goals
  - Confidence in readiness for the program

Summary

- Passion for computer science ignited in high school
- Influential experiences: summer internship, app development
- Academic achievements in advanced courses & research
- Aspiration: contribute to technological advancements
- XYZ University offers an ideal growth environment

Additional Notes

- Research more about specific faculty and facilities at XYZ University
- Explore opportunities for collaboration and community engagement

Figure 5.5: Cornell Notes

Follow these steps to use this method for the SOP writing process:

a. **Set up the Cornell Notes layout**: Draw a line about 2.5 inches from the left side of your paper, creating a vertical margin. Leave the right side for later use. Write the topic or question related to your SOP at the top.

b. **Take notes during brainstorming**: Start brainstorming ideas, examples, and key points related to your SOP. As you brainstorm, write down your thoughts in the main note-taking section to the right of the vertical margin. Use bullet points to capture your ideas.

c. **Use the vertical margin for cues and prompts**: As you brainstorm, use the vertical margin on the left to write down cues or prompts related to each idea or key point. These cues will help trigger your memory and provide a quick overview of the content when you review your notes later.

d. **Review and reflect**: After the brainstorming session, review your notes. Pay attention to the cues in the left margin and try to elaborate on the ideas and points in the main note-taking section. Add any additional thoughts or connections that come to mind.

e. **Identify main themes or sections**: Based on your reviewed notes, identify the main themes or sections that will structure your SOP. These themes can become the headings or subheadings in your document.

f. **Transfer notes to an outline or draft**: Using the main themes or sections as a guide, create an outline or draft for your SOP. Expand upon the ideas and points from your Cornell Notes, providing detailed explanation, anecdotes, examples, and transition between sections.

By incorporating cues and prompts in the Cornell Notes, you can easily retrieve and expand on your thoughts. Remember to customize the Cornell Notes layout to suit your needs and preferences while maintaining focus on the topic of your SOP.

6

FLOW OF SOP

Whether you are a prospective bachelor's student, a master's applicant, or a PhD aspirant, the general structure and intent of the SOP remain the same, but there are some key differences in their content and focus that are essential to understand in order to decide the flow and outline of your SOP.

★ **Undergraduate SOP** emphasizes the student's academic exploration and goals. It centers on why the applicant has chosen a particular field of study and what they hope to achieve academically during their undergraduate years.

★ **Graduate SOP** focuses on the applicant's specific research interests and potential areas of specialization within their chosen field of study. It emphasizes the student's readiness to engage in advanced research and scholarly pursuits.

★ **Doctorate SOP** may include an original research proposal. Ph.D. applicants present potential research topics or questions they intend to explore during their doctoral studies, showcasing their ability to contribute meaningfully through research.

With all the information and knowledge gathered from the previous chapters, it's time to discuss the flow of the SOP. There are mainly two ways to narrate your story:

1. Chronological Order
2. Reverse Chronological Order

The former is more suitable for college students, while the latter is apt for working professionals with substantial work experience.

1. **Chronological Order**

Figure 6.1: Flow of SOP – Chronological Order

a. **Childhood Aspirations:** Did a life-changing event occur during your childhood? Did you face any financial hardship or educational barrier? Or did you have a teacher in school who inspired you? If yes, then it may be a good idea to start your essay with that particular, highly interesting, and aspirational piece of information.

Be mindful that many universities would want you to keep the tone intellectual, professional, and mature; thereby, discouraging the use of childhood stories in SOPs.

b. **High School and College Experience:** Demonstrate attributes like curiosity, creativity, teamwork, and the ability to think independently, as well as enthusiasm for learning, through your high school and college-level activities. This may include entrance exams, live projects, science fairs, hackathons, competitions, research publications, and extracurricular activities, to name a few.

c. **Professional Experience:** Internships, part-time jobs, full-time jobs, or any hands-on skills gained at a company/organization under supervision count towards professional experience. Industry-hardened skills and experiential learning, in your field of interest, are highly appreciated by universities across the globe. It manifests your ability to thrive and excel in a cross-functional setting outside your classroom.

d. **Career Goals:** Prospective Master's and PhD students are advised to articulate their professional objectives, both short-term (right after graduation) and long-term (10 years down the line), unambiguously in their statement of purpose. Although undergraduate applicants may not have a clear picture of their future at this point of time, they should still exhibit a certain inclination towards either research, academia, or job.

e. Why this University: It is now time to change perspective and explain why the University would be a good match for you. Bolster your argument by mentioning professors' names, specific courses, electives, research labs, student organizations, and other distinct program features that pique your interest. Research thoroughly the University's website, follow their social media accounts, and network with professors/alumni to gather this information.

2. Reverse Chronological Order

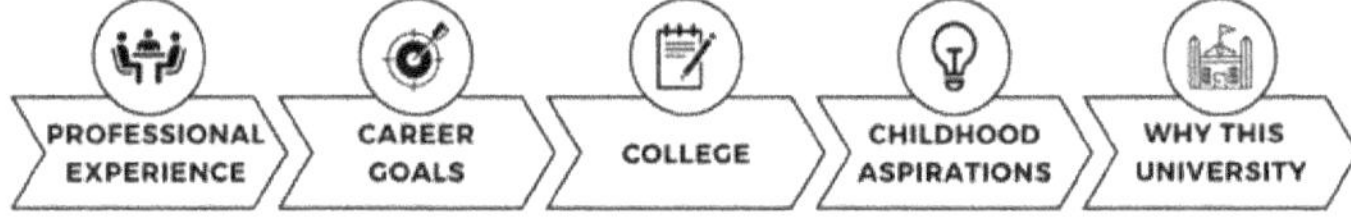

Figure 6.2: Flow of SOP – Reverse Chronological Order

a. Professional Experience: Start by talking about your career aspirations and previous work experience, and how they relate to your desired field of study. Showcase your enthusiasm, proficiency, and expertise in the chosen program by highlighting the relevant work and projects you have completed throughout your career. Persuade the Admission Committee that you have the potential to make a valuable contribution to their ongoing initiatives (and to the university) by leveraging your industry-hardened skills.

b. Career Goals: Set high aspirations and proudly articulate your professional objectives, built upon your extensive work background. For instance, if you currently hold the position of a project manager, dream big, aiming to become an entrepreneur or CEO/CTO of a global organization. Similarly, if you're an astrobiologist, you should strive for the utmost heights, both figuratively and literally, by envisioning yourself as an Astronaut.

c. College (Undergraduate Tenure): The focus of this layout is on your work life; therefore, you may dedicate just one (or at the most two) paragraph(s) to your college performance and activities. Highlight distinctive events from your student life, like real-world projects, podium finishes in any sport or competition, state/national level achievements, to support your personal and professional goals.

d. Childhood Aspirations: Include childhood motivations only if they add an extra dimension to your personality and to your story.

e. Why this University: Here, in addition to the points mentioned for the Chronological Order, explore the various companies that actively recruit from this university during campus placement events and relate this to your career objectives. Additionally, you can cite examples of few accomplished alumni of this institution.

7

CRAFTING THE BLUEPRINT

Le Corbusier is renowned for building Chandigarh, India's first meticulously planned city, in a remarkably short period of three years. This noteworthy achievement can be attributed to his efforts during the initial stages, where he dedicated his time to designing and refining the blueprints. The same principle applies to SOP writing. Developing a well-structured blueprint for your SOP will expedite the essay drafting process.

Following is a sample outline for the student from the Affinity Wall example who wants to pursue a Master in Pharmacy from UNC Chapel Hill.

Sample Blueprint

1. Introduction

- Discuss the impact of the Covid-19 pandemic, including the tragic loss of lives caused by the Corona Virus

- Highlight the decisive role played by pharmaceutical companies and their collaborative endeavors to expedite the development of Covid vaccines

- Draw motivation from this experience and express aspiration to contribute to similar initiatives in the future

2. Academic

- Discuss relevant college coursework and research paper on Cosmetics

- Dedicate one paragraph to the experiential learning from internships at AIIMS and PQR Lab; compare the experience of working in a hospital vs. an industry/lab setup

3. Extracurricular & Co-curricular Activities

- Share non-academic accomplishments, such as the challenges encountered and overcome along the way to the National level Badminton tournaments

- Showcase leadership skills by stating roles such as House Captain and President of the Student Cell

- Substantiate commitment to community service by highlighting the volunteer work at a school for children with special needs

4. Goals

- Aspire to pursue PhD in Pharmacology upon graduation

- Work as a researcher at Pfizer or Astrazeneca, in the long run

5. University Specific Paragraph

- Discuss Prof. Jacqui, Prof. Scott, Prof. Tyler's work in pharmacy and related fields at UNC Chapel Hill's Eshelman School of Pharmacy

- Emphasize on unique aspects of the program such as CIPhER Seminars, Center for Nanotechnology in Drug Delivery (CNDD), and Rapidly Emerging Antiviral Drug Development Initiative

- Talk about specialized pathways namely Global Pharmacy Scholars, Rural Pharmacy Health Certificate, and RASP and link it with overall career objective

6. Conclusion

- With the dedicated efforts of researchers and scientists in the realm of Cancer Vaccines, there exist vast prospects for meaningful engagement and contribution in this area.

- UNC Chapel Hill has a rich history of pioneering innovations in the field of pharmaceutical sciences; support this with examples.

- In closing, UNC Chapel Hill is the ideal launchpad to achieve the career goals and create a positive impact on a global scale.

Create your own blueprint here:

Create your own blueprint here:

8

ESSAY WRITING RULES

In this chapter, we will go over four essential Essay-Writing rules. While this book does not aim at teaching the basics, I have included some helpful resources in Chapter 13 for polishing your creative writing skills. These books can aid in boosting grammar and widening the gamut of vocabulary.

1. Maintain the flow

When it comes to writing essays, a paragraph is the fundamental building block. Paragraphs can vary in length depending on the ideas you are trying to convey, but they should always focus on one main point. As you craft each paragraph, consider what idea you want your reader to grasp and make sure to convey it in the first sentence to capture their attention.

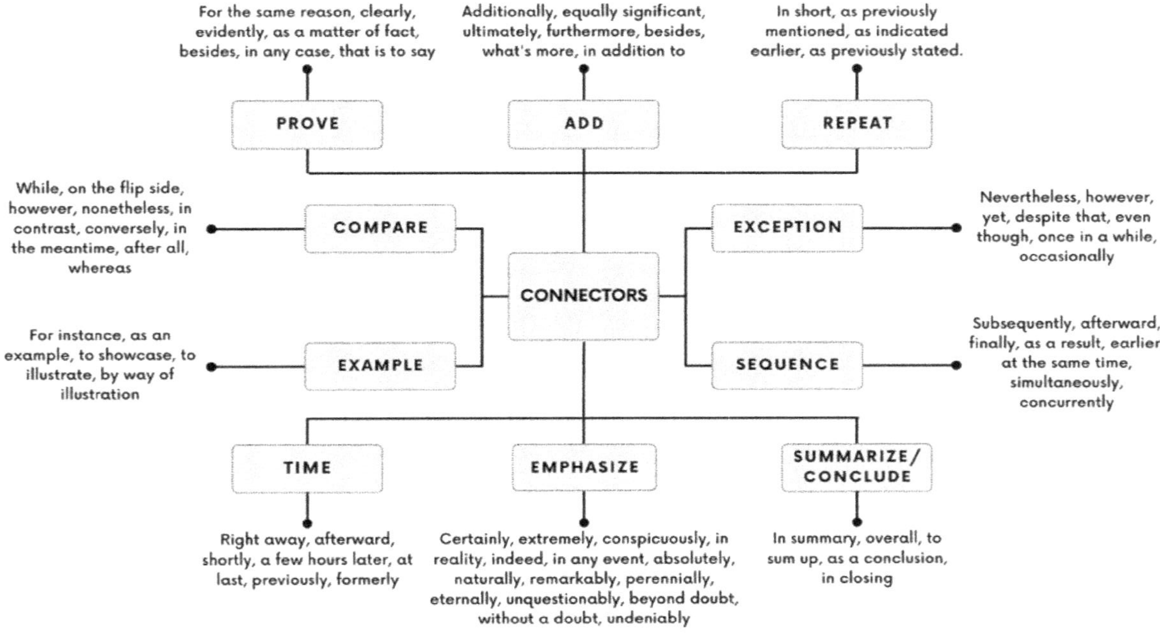

Figure 8.1: Connecting Words

To maintain a smooth and logical flow in your essay, it is essential to use connecting words to link your ideas together. Imagine constructing a wall without any cement. How would you build it and raise the structure if there is no glue to hold the bricks together? Similarly, while writing an essay, sentences and paragraphs should be connected with the help of transition words, creating a fabric woven seamlessly with different threads of the essay prompt. *Figure 8.1* shows various connecting words (but not limited to) that you can use to maintain the flow of your essay.

Example of a Paragraph without any connectors:

, during a mandatory internship in my final semester, I was compelled to resign due to my mother's deteriorating health, which demanded my immediate attention and care. , I couldn't submit my internship report, which affected my grades. While my grades may not reflect my true potential, a closer look at my background and accomplishments reveals my unfaltering dedication to this field.

, I am proud to have published two research papers, demonstrating my capacity to contribute to the scientific community. , my passion project in Bioinformatics showcases my commitment to the field, as I tirelessly pursued innovative solutions and explored novel avenues. , I humbly

request the admission committee to look beyond my academic setbacks and recognize the depth of my determination, accomplishments, and potential to excel in USC's demanding Molecular Biology program.

Now let's add some transition words and see the difference:

***Unfortunately**, during a mandatory internship in my final semester, I was compelled to resign due to my mother's deteriorating health, which demanded my immediate attention and care. **Consequently**, I couldn't submit my internship report, which **subsequently** affected my grades. While my grades may not reflect my true potential, a closer look at my background and accomplishments reveals my unfaltering dedication to this field.*

***Nevertheless**, I am proud to have published two research papers, demonstrating my capacity to contribute to the scientific community. **Additionally**, my passion project in Bioinformatics showcases my commitment to the field, as I tirelessly pursued innovative solutions and explored novel avenues. **Therefore**, I humbly request the admission committee to look beyond my academic setbacks and recognize the depth of my determination, passion, and potential to excel in USC's demanding Molecular Biology program.*

2.   Paint a vivid picture

Use descriptive imagery and sensory details to engage the reader. Demonstrate your achievements through concrete examples or anecdotes. Admission committees are curious to know about your personal journey, challenges, and growth, so don't just list your accomplishments without context. It should neither sound too mechanical nor too overachieving. Therefore, it is pertinent to insert emotions and expressions into your writing and make a connection with the reader.

One way to craft vivid imagery is to:

a. introduce something out-of-the-ordinary
b. incorporate conflicts and struggles and the steps taken to overcome them
c. utilize concrete details like facts; abstract details such as skills learned, and qualities showcased; and examples to support your story

Ultimately, an impressive statement of purpose is one that conveys your unique perspective and interpretation of your experiences. Ensure a cohesive narration by weaving together all paragraphs into one interesting story.

Let's take a look at the following two essay excerpts:

Excerpt 1:

In the summer of 2018, my family and I set out on an unforgettable expedition to the enchanting region of Kashmir. During our visit, we explored several historical and cultural gems. We marveled at the awe-inspiring architecture of ancient Mughal gardens, admired the breathtaking landscapes of the Dal Lake, and ventured into the picturesque valleys of Pahalgam and Gulmarg. Our trip to Kashmir was a transformative experience, as it deepened my fascination with diverse cultures and opened up new avenues of understanding. As I immersed myself in the region's rich culture and history, my resolve to pursue a career in medicine grew stronger.

Excerpt 2:

"I've discovered my Ikigai," I murmured as I gazed out from a vantage point, where one side revealed awe-inspiring, snow-capped mountains against the backdrop of a serene, clear-blue lake, while the other side presented a disheartening scene of an endless queue of patients outside a makeshift clinic, attended to by a lone healthcare practitioner. This striking contrast, witnessed during my journey through the picturesque valleys of Kashmir, unveiled my true purpose – the missing piece in my Ikigai Venn Diagram – to make a difference in the lives of people around the world. My journey had taken on a higher purpose – one that merged my passion for medicine, my desire to help others, and my commitment to working with organizations like "World Health Organization" to create a positive impact across the world.

Which of the above two essay excerpts do you find more impressive?

I would go with *Excerpt 2,* as it provides a well-articulated narrative where the writer has experienced some emotional struggle during their trip and interweaves it with their desire to become a doctor. *Excerpt 1* lacks correlation between the narrator's travel experience and their career goals; nothing extraordinary happened that demonstrates the writer's motivation to overcome challenges or resolve conflicts through a medicine degree. *Excerpt 2* sounds more intelligent and structured as it draws inspiration from a book to describe their life's calling.

Think of an experience that had a life-changing impact on you and try to describe it below:

____

____

____

____

____

____

____

____

____

____

Excerpt 3:

As a student coordinator, I assumed a pivotal role in arranging a workshop, a field trip for senior year students, and an industrial visit for my peers. Also, as an active community member, I regularly engaged in fundraising events and successfully collected substantial funds to aid children afflicted with the severe skin disease, Leprosy. These hands-on experiences have ignited a deeper sense of confidence within me.

Feedback: Readers will easily forget what they have read in the above paragraph since the details and particulars of the events are missing.

Revised Excerpt 3 with concrete and abstract details: *As a student coordinator of College of Computer Science, I assumed a pivotal role in arranging an "R Programming" workshop by data science professionals, a company visit to Google Bangalore Campus for 35 final year students, and an industrial trip to Amazon FC Bhiwandi Center for my peers. Taking charge and orchestrating these beneficial programs for my colleagues brought me an immense sense of achievement and contentment.*

Furthermore, as an active volunteer of Alert-Citizens, I have regularly engaged in fundraising events and successfully collected 70,000 rupees to help 11 children avoid permanently losing their limbs to a severe case of Leprosy. Engaging in volunteer initiatives boosted my morale as each smiling face contributed to a growing sense of confidence in me.

Think of a project or assignment that was successfully executed by you. Now, use the blank space below to describe it using concrete details like number of participants, place, outcome, etc. and abstract results such as skills learned, qualities showcased, your growth as an individual, etc.

____

____

____

____

____

____

____

____

____

____

____

3. Diction and Style of Writing

Who is your target audience? Who will be reading your SOP?

Let's say there are two items on a restaurant's menu as shown below and you're asked to order any one. Which one will you pick?

- Verdant Symphony with Quinoa Du Jour
- Seasonal Vegetable and Quinoa Salad

The first one might resonate more with those who appreciate gourmet dining but the second one is named to be approachable and appealing to a wider audience without requiring specialized culinary knowledge. Both items are identical, just that they are marketed differently.

Similarly, your language should strike a balance between formality that showcases your expertise in the field and simplicity that ensures that your ideas can be comprehended by a general audience.

Example: *Participating in the development of the COVID-19 vaccine was an extraordinary and humbling experience that immersed me in the realm of immunology and vaccine research. Our project aim was to create a safe and effective vaccine against the SARS-CoV-2 virus. Extensive molecular biology work involved identifying key* *viral antigens and employing recombinant DNA technology to produce antigen constructs for vaccine development. The vaccine candidates were subjected to rigorous in-vitro and in-vivo testing, assessing their ability to induce a robust immune response while maintaining safety profiles. The technical data collected during the preclinical studies revealed the vaccine's ability to elicit strong antibody responses against the spike protein and T-cell activation.*

Revised Example: *Participating in the development of the COVID-19 vaccine was an extraordinary and humbling experience that immersed me in the realm of immunology and vaccine research. Utilizing cutting-edge technology, we identified fundamental components of the SARS-CoV-2 virus and developed a potential vaccine. Thorough testing in both laboratory settings and animal models ensured its efficacy and safety. The technical data collected during the preclinical studies revealed the vaccine's ability to produce strong antibody responses against the spike protein and T-cell activation.*

Please note that the first writeup is perfectly fine when applying for research or doctoral positions, as PhD aspirants are expected to have sound and scientific knowledge of their field.

Now, consider a food critic who tastes a dish at a restaurant. The critic forms a subjective impression of the chef's skills and the restaurant's overall experience based on the subtle flavors and presentation of the dish.

Likewise, admission officers form subjective impressions of the applicants and their suitability for admission based on the subtle emotional nuances and qualities expressed in the writing.

Here are some tips to make your SOP appear more presentable:

- Avoid the use of slang, text message language, or informal teenage expressions
- Steer clear of abbreviations and contractions
- Ensure that your spell check is set to U.S. English when applying to US Universities
- Make it presentable by selecting the right font size, style, and alignment. (I personally prefer to 'Justify' my text)
- Use proper nouns/common nouns instead of pronouns and articles, wherever possible

With this, lets read the example given below and point out the usage of informal tone.

Non-professional tone Example: *I had an amazing time participating in the "Design Futuristic Vehicle" competition. It was all about creating a super cool car of the future with other students from different schools. We had to come up with new and smart ideas for the vehicle ASAP. Our team worked really hard, spending a lot of time thinking and making a prototype. Our car was* *super advanced, running on electricity with a powerful battery, and it could go really fast, up to 180 km/h. The design was made to be smooth and efficient, saving energy. We even made it so the car could drive itself using smart sensors. Everything was hunky dory. While we didn't win the top prize, the experience was fantastic, and it made me want to keep working on cool and sustainable ideas for the cars of the future.*

Revised Example: *Participating in the "Design Futuristic Vehicle" competition was an enthralling journey that allowed me to explore my passion for engineering and innovation. The competition brought together aspiring engineers from various universities, with over 20 teams and 100 participants. We were tasked with designing a cutting-edge vehicle of the future, incorporating advanced technologies and sustainable solutions. Our team spent countless hours brainstorming, prototyping, and refining our design. The sleek and aerodynamic design reduced drag and enhanced efficiency, resulting in a reduced energy consumption of just 10 kWh per 100 km. Additionally, we integrated autonomous driving capabilities, leveraging advanced sensors and artificial intelligence algorithms for seamless navigation and obstacle avoidance. Although we did not secure the top prize, the experience was invaluable, and we were proud of our achievement. The competition sparked a lasting passion for* *sustainable engineering and inspired us to continue pushing the boundaries of automotive innovation in the pursuit of a greener and more efficient future.*

4.   Strong Introduction and Conclusion

An essay that begins with a riveting opening statement, enticing the reader to delve further, and ends with a powerful closing that leaves the reader pondering and reflecting is considered a truly impactful piece of writing.

Most of the students struggle with the opening and closing of the SOP, since those are the two trickiest and most important paragraphs of an essay and in the excitement (or nervousness) of writing something unique and unprecedented, they often miss the essence – *why are you writing this SOP? What do you want to convey to the admission committee?*

Example Introduction

"Passion is the bridge that takes you from pain to change."

The words of the renowned painter Frida Kahlo resonate deeply with me, as they perfectly capture my personal journey into the realm of science and research.

It was during the first year of my medicine degree when an earth-shattering event occurred, when unfortunately, my teenage sister experienced vision loss due to glaucoma. *Witnessing her suffering had a profound emotional impact on me. Initially, I felt distressed, but my ache soon transformed into a powerful motivation to seek a solution for her.*

Example Conclusion

The burning desire to assist my ailing sister has propelled me to delve into the extensive knowledge within the field of ophthalmology, revealing my genuine passion and calling, just as Kahlo once asserted. If granted admission, I am willing to go the extra mile to make a significant and impactful contribution to the ongoing Glaucoma research at Imperial.

9

PARSING THE PROMPT

A Statement of Purpose prompt is a set of instructions given to applicants of graduate programs or other academic pursuits, outlining what they should include in their statement of purpose. Analyzing an SOP prompt involves breaking it down into its component parts and evaluating each element to ensure that the instructions are clear, concise, and comprehensible.

Example: University of Michigan Ann Arbor (UMich) MS SOP prompt [xxv]

The Academic Statement of Purpose should be concise, typically no more than two pages, a well-written statement about your academic and research background, your career goals, and how this graduate program will help you meet your career and educational objectives. You can include the information about potential research labs and faculty advisors in this statement.

Here is how you can analyze the SOP prompt by parsing its different components:

✓ **should be concise, typically no more than two pages**

Compose a succinct and lucid statement of purpose that spans two pages. The term *typically* denotes that if your SOP exceeds the two-page limit by, say, four or five lines, that might be acceptable. Nonetheless, it is advisable that your SOP conforms to the specified page, word, or character count. In many instances, when you must copy-paste your SOP into the university application portal, the extra words or characters will be automatically truncated by the system. As a result, please ensure that your essay falls well within the specified constraints to avoid any last-minute panic.

✓ **well-written statement**

Ensure that your SOP is devoid of typos, spelling errors, syntax errors, and grammatical mistakes. It should be well-organized, with clear paragraph breaks and sentence structure. Personally, I prefer to use the *Justify* alignment rather than the *Left* alignment, as it lends a more polished and refined look to my writing.

✓ **academic and research background**

Background refers to those aspects of your academic and professional work and projects that are related to your intended field of study and future career. Feel free to talk about your research work, it can be any research work under the guidance of some professor or subject matter expert or any research project done independently.

✓ **career goals**

Reiterating from previous chapters, it's imperative to talk about your career goals, be it establishing an e-commerce startup, working as a professor in academia, or practicing as a Sports Nutritionist. Career Goals should include both your short-term and long-term goals and the steps you will take to achieve them.

✓ **how this graduate program will help you meet your career and educational objectives**

Thoroughly investigate the university website to understand its uniqueness and how you intend to spend your time at this graduate school. Your SOP should clearly demonstrate your familiarity with the department, school, and program to which you are seeking admission. This can be illustrated through the academic courses, projects, electives, internships, research, and extracurriculars you wish to pursue at the university. Integrate these pursuits into your professional and career goals description, as stated in the preceding paragraph.

✓ **potential research labs and faculty advisors in this statement**

Including the names of potential labs and faculty advisors you aspire to work at/with is always a good idea. It shows your knowledge of the program as well as your deep-seated interest in your intended major. And this university has specifically asked for it. So go for it! Do not hesitate to email the professors or talk to an alumnus to gather relevant information.

This is how you parse the SOP prompt. As our next exercise, I have included some SOP prompts by different universities. Try to break down these prompts into small, manageable parts and make a note of pointers to talk about for each of these components.

1. **Doctor of Education Leadership (Ed.L.D.) – Harvard University** [ix]

> *What lived experiences have contributed to your commitment to education? What do you view as your most significant professional accomplishment(s) and your most significant professional failure(s) to date? How did they inform your development? What issues would you like to tackle in your career as a system-level leader in education? How do you envision yourself affecting significant change in the American Pre-K-12 education sector?*

____

____

____

____

---

2. MSc in Public Policy Research – University of Oxford [xxvi]

Personal Statement (maximum 800 words)

You should explain why you want to do the MSc, how your experience to date prepares you for the course, and how the MSc would enhance your future plans. Please also outline your specific policy interests and the skills and experience you would bring to the classroom.

If possible, please ensure that the word count is clearly displayed on the document.

---

3. Master of Public Health – Bloomberg School of Public Health, Johns Hopkins University [xi]

The Statement of Purpose and Objectives is the applicant's opportunity to share with the admission committee their passion for public health, their interest in the program and research projects, and any other relevant information not included in the rest of the application.

---

4. MS in Education Data Science – Stanford University [xvi]

Your typed, single-spaced statement of purpose should be between one and two pages with 12-point font and regular, one-inch margins. Describe your reasons for applying, your preparation for this field of study, why our program is a good fit for you, your future career goals, and other aspects of your background and interests that might aid the admissions committee in evaluating your aptitude and motivation for graduate study.

---

5. MBA – Anderson School of Management, U.C.L.A. [xix]

UCLA Anderson seeks to develop transformative leaders who think fearlessly, drive change, and share success. We believe the ability to persevere is an essential component of effective leadership. Please share an example from your personal or professional life where you demonstrated perseverance to accomplish a significant goal or milestone. (250 words maximum)

---

6. PhD in Geological and Planetary Science – California Institute of Technology (CalTech) [iv]

Provide a brief statement of your scientific and professional interests and objectives. Include a description of your past accomplishments that are not evident from the examination of other documents submitted. Report, if applicable, on any research in progress. The statement must be written by the applicant in English. It must not be written in another language and translated for the applicant by another person.

---

7. **Master of Arts Program in Social Sciences (MAPSS) – University of Chicago** [xvii]

   A 2–4-page Candidate Statement, outlining your research interest, relevant training, prior academic distinctions, and your fit for 2 or 3 UChicago faculty members.

8. PhD in Bioinformatics – Max Planck Institute of Immunobiology and Epigenetics [xii]

Two-page motivational letter. Please use your own words. The motivational letter should highlight your major experimental experiences and how they have prepared you for a PhD with IMPRS-IEM. Please explain why you are interested in specific labs and what you hope to gain from them during your doctoral studies that will contribute to your future professional goals.

---

9. Motivation letter – MSc in Engineering and Policy Analysis – TU Delft [vi]

A clear and relevant essay in English (1,000 – 1,500 words) addressing the following:

- *Your motivation for choosing this MSc programme.*
- *Why you are interested in TU Delft and what you expect to find here.*
- *If this MSc programme has specialisation(s), which specialisation interests you the most and why?*
- *Describe your hypothetical thesis project: what kind of project would you prefer? What would you want to explore? Please limit your answer to three possible topics. Summarise in a maximum of 250 words, your BSc thesis work or final assignment/project. Please include information about the workload.*

____

____

____

____

____

____

____

10. BS/MS in Computer Science & Engineering: University of Washington [xxvii]

Statement of Purpose. Recommended length: 750-1000 words. Topics to address include: (1) Why are you interested in pursuing a combined BS/MS? (2) What specific aspects of the program interest you, such as areas of study? (3) What makes you a good candidate for this program?

____

____

____

____

____

____

____

10

University Research

Enough about *'why you are a good fit for the university;'* now it is time to reveal *'why the university is a good fit for you.'*

Generally, students who aspire to study abroad have a preferred or dream university in mind, but the majority of them lack a clear understanding of why they want to study there. The most common responses I receive include:

- recommendations from distant relatives
- presence of research facilities
- friends applying to the same University
- University's proximity to Silicon Valley
- impressive podcast by one of the University's professors
- exciting campus life

While these motivations may seem reasonable, they are not sufficient to impress the Admission Committee. To demonstrate genuine interest in studying at a particular university, it is important to delve deeper. Here are five unique selling points (USPs) that you should thoroughly research on the university's website and include in your Statement of Purpose (SOP):

1. **Subjects/Electives Offered**: Look for distinctive courses offered by the university in your field of interest. Include the names of these courses and explain why you are eager to study them.

2. **Research Labs and Projects**: Merely stating the presence of research facilities isn't impressive. Review the research labs and ongoing projects at the university. Establish a meaningful connection between your previous projects and the research endeavors, undertaken at the university, and showcase your genuine enthusiasm for making valuable contributions to research activities.

3. **Professor Names**: Identify two to three professors whose guidance you would like to seek for your research project. You may also express your wholehearted interest in working under their aegis by initiating contact via email or social media messaging.

4. **Internships and Campus Placement**: Explore the companies or organizations that visit the university to hire students for part-time or full-time roles. Linking

your decision to study at the university with your career goals will strengthen your application.

5. **Student Clubs and Organizations**: Research and specify two to three student clubs you would like to join during your graduate studies. Involvement in extracurricular activities and community service not only offers respite from academic pressures but also enables you to reciprocate to the university and its student community.

Including precise factual data about the University and the prospective program in your SOP will demonstrate your deep-rooted interest and motivation in studying at the university and increase your visibility to the Admission Committee.

Example of University-specific paragraph

After building a solid foundation in my chosen field of study, my aspiration is now to complement it with cutting-edge and avant-garde skills through a PhD in Anthropology at Princeton University. My primary interest lies in exploring the complexity of human interaction within the society and its impact on their overall cultures. I am deeply drawn to the prospect of engaging in the study of Japan Anthropology, Social Theory and East Asia, and Language and Subjectivity, while also participating in intellectual discussions involving peers with diverse backgrounds and distinguished professors.

I find great inspiration in the research conducted by Prof. ABC, whose work aligns perfectly with my academic pursuits. He has graciously agreed to consider me as a Research Assistant if I am accepted into this program. Having previously worked on similar research problems, I am enthusiastic about conducting substantial research under his guidance and mentorship.

Research and write down the points that you would like to include in your SOP

____

____

____

____

____

____

____

____

____

____

____

____

____

____

11

COMMON MISTAKES

So far, we have covered a lot of ground concerning the Statement of Purpose, including its definition and significance, the essay writing cycle, two primary types of flow, sample blueprints, various essay writing rules, and some creative brainstorming methods. It's understandable if all this information has left you feeling overwhelmed. Take a deep breath, make *Jazz* hands, stretch a bit, and review some common mistakes to dodge when writing your essay, making it more concise, crisp, and engrossing.

If you find that you have inadvertently made any of the following mistakes in your SOP, don't worry; you can always refer back to this section at any stage during your writing process and make the required changes.

1.   Purple Prose

The term *Purple Prose* was created by the renowned poet Horace to describe an excessively elaborate and pompous writing style. To better understand this concept, let's draw a parallel with car body work. In this analogy, purple prose would be like making extravagant modifications to a car, such as adding unnecessary features, to make it appear more visually appealing or luxurious.

Consider fitting a station wagon or a compact hatchback with a large, sleekly designed rear spoiler. It's similar to embellishing a well-written essay with too many adjectives and showy comparisons. Just as this excessive language can overwhelm the simplicity and charm of the story, the practical design of the wagon is overshadowed by a spoiler more suited for high-performance sports cars. It's as if the car is attempting to be a sporty vehicle when, in reality, it's meant for everyday use. This results in the car looking odd and out of place, as if it's trying too hard to be something it isn't.

Similarly, using complex and overly decorative language in writing doesn't necessarily indicate author's intelligence or knowledge. In fact, it typically confuses the reader, sounds unnatural, and fills the text with unnecessary words.

Example 1:

As a final-year mechanical engineering student, my academic journey unfolds amidst a rich tapestry of coursework that resembles nothing short of an intricate symphony of knowledge. Each course, a unique note in this grand composition of engineering mastery, leads me through the labyrinthine corridors of thermodynamics, quantum mechanics, and differential equations. I navigate this academic odyssey with resolute determination, punctuating it with the harmonious resonance of materials science and fluid dynamics. However, amid this intellectual crescendo, my pièce de résistance emerges—the capstone project. It represents a magnum opus that weaves together the threads of theoretical erudition and practical finesse, resulting in an engineering marvel that promises to outshine the stars themselves and etch my name into the annals of mechanical engineering history.

Problem: Above example is packed with unwanted adjectives and adverbs, which makes the text wordy and difficult to comprehend.

Edited Text: *As a final year mechanical engineering student, I've been navigating challenging courses in thermodynamics, quantum mechanics, and differential equations, along with the practical aspects of materials science and fluid dynamics. Nevertheless, the highlight of my academic journey is the capstone project, 'Chainless Bicycles', where I aim to combine my theoretical knowledge and practical skills to create something remarkable in the field of mechanical* *engineering. This project represents my dedication and ambition in this field.*

Example 2:

Embarking on a corporate job experience can be described as a Bunyanesque expedition, navigating through a labyrinth of challenges and opportunities. As a Sales Associate, I proffer my precocious skills and expertise in the dynamic world of business. Being a crackerjack employee, I stand statuesque, embodying a quintessential representation of devotion and competence. The corporate landscape is paradigmatic, demanding highfalutin strategies and transcendental thinking to stay ahead. It is an extraordinaire journey, where the cardinal goal is to shine resplendently among peers, showcasing innovative ideation and pauciloquent communication. However, amidst the adumbration of success, the solivagant nature of decision-making may lead to occasional tergiversation. Nevertheless, with determination and resilience, the corporate job experience provides invaluable growth and learning opportunities that shape me into an accomplished professional.

Try editing the above text by replacing the purple prose with a less-flowery language.

Use of dictionary is permitted since even MS Word failed to recognize some of these words and gave me a red line (sigh).

Be natural and refrain from pretense. Your writing should mirror your true personality and character. Avoid using over-accessorized writing style that appears out of place and confusing.

2. Plagiarism

Copying from any book or online resource, including the university website, is considered plagiarism. Avoid plagiarism in essays to ensure academic integrity, maintain ethical standards, avoid legal and academic consequences (such as getting your application rejected), and produce high-quality work.

It is highly recommended to run your documents through online plagiarism checker tools and make sure your essays are 100% original. If you are using quotes or research excerpts in your SOP, do not forget to cite the author or the source.

3. Nominalization

Imagine you're watching a thrilling action movie, where the hero is performing all sorts of incredible stunts and dynamic actions. It's like a live, heart-pounding performance that keeps you on the edge of your seat.

Now, let's say you take a screenshot of one of those intense moments from the movie. While the image still captures some of the excitement, it's not as thrilling as watching the action unfold in real time.

In writing, when you use nominalization, it's similar to taking that snapshot from the movie. You're turning dynamic, action-packed verbs into static, lifeless nouns. And the result is that your writing becomes less engaging and more verbose.

Example 1: *The discussion of the issue **led to a resolution** of the conflict.*

Edited Sentence: *The discussion of the issue **resolved** the conflict.*

Example 2: *The **analysis of the data resulted in a** clear **understanding** of the trends.*

Edited Sentence: ***Analyzing** the data **revealed** clear trends.*

Try to identify the nouns in the sentences below and replace it with the right verb:

- *I undertook an internship with Microsoft.*
- *I made a decision to pursue a medical degree.*
- *The implementation of the plan required careful consideration of various factors.*
- *The investigation of the matter revealed significant discrepancies in the accounts.*
- *The presentation of the findings provided a comprehensive overview of the research outcomes.*

____

____

____

____

____

____

____

____

____

____

____

____

____

____

4. Cliches

Cliches are overused expressions that can make your writing seem unoriginal and lackluster.

Examples:
   a. *Ever since I was a child, I have always been passionate about ...*
   b. *I want to make a difference in the world.*
   c. *I have always been fascinated by the way things work.*
   d. *My experiences have made me the person I am today.*
   e. *I have always been interested in helping others.*

While these statements may reflect your genuine feelings, they are overused and can make you sound unoriginal. Strive for a unique and personal voice in your SOP to make it stand exceptional.

5. Weak Verbs

Verbs serve as the fundamental building block of a sentence. Just as a painter chooses strong, vivid colors to create a captivating work of art, a writer should choose strong verbs to create compelling and vivid writing. Weak verbs are like the faded colors you'd want to avoid when trying to make your writing more engaging and impactful.

Example: *She **did well** in the race.*

Edited Sentence: *She **excelled** in the race.*

Most of the time, we tend to compensate for these faded, washed-out colors with extra decorations and embellishments (adverbs). However, this can clutter your paintings instead of enhancing it. So, rather than relying on numerous adverbs to enhance your weak verbs, it's more effective to choose powerful verbs to make your writing, vivid and captivating.

Example: *She **walked slowly** across the room.*

Edited Sentence: *She **ambled** across the room.*

Identify and replace the weak verbs in the sentences below with strong verbs:

- *She put on a beautiful dress.*
- *They had a meeting for brainstorming event ideas.*
- *She made a promise to take him to garden.*
- *They ate quickly at the restaurant.*
- *Mark spoke quietly in the library.*

____

____

____

____

____

____

____

____

____

____

____

____

6. Religious Motivations

Generally, it's always a good idea to avoid religious motivations in your Statement of Purpose because it is a personal belief that may not be relevant or interesting to the admission committee.

Examples:
a. *I feel called by God to pursue a career in medicine and use my skills to serve others.*
b. *Religion has taught me the importance of social justice and I want to use my education to make a positive impact in the world.*

c. *I believe that my purpose in life is to spread the word of God through my academic achievements.*

Including such remarks (whether on a serious note or in a lighthearted manner) may potentially offend members of the admission committee who have different religious preferences or no beliefs at all. Therefore, it's best to focus on your academic and professional goals and how you plan to contribute to your field of study rather than incorporating religious motivations into your SOP.

7. **Sticky Sentences**

For all the coffee (or tea) lovers, what happens when you add too much water to your decoction? It dilutes the beverage's flavor, making it weak and less enjoyable. In writing, sticky sentences are formed when you use too many unnecessary words or filler words that don't add value to the sentence. These extra words *dilute* the overall impact of your writing, making it less appealing and engaging. Just as you want your Cuppa Joe to have a strong, rich flavor, you want your writing to be clear and concise, free from the unnecessary words that make sentences *sticky*. By eliminating sticky sentences, you ensure that your writing retains its strength and impact, just like a perfectly brewed cup of coffee.

Example 1: *While pursuing my undergraduate studies, I came across various complex electrical engineering problems, and I found them to be highly interesting and engaging in nature, which* *piqued my curiosity and drove me to delve deeper into the subject matter.*

Edited Sentence: *During my undergraduate tenure, I encountered complex electrical engineering problems that not only captured my interest but also fueled my curiosity, motivating me to explore the subject in depth.*

Example 2: *Due to my longstanding fascination with the field of political science, I have always been deeply intrigued by the intricate workings of various political systems and their impact on societies around the world.*

Edited Sentence: *My longstanding fascination with political science stems from a deep interest in the complex dynamics of political systems and their global societal implications.*

Identify the stickiness in the sentences below and make them crisper and clearer. Also note down the number of words/characters you save in the process.

- From an early age, I have possessed a strong interest in the field of economics, and I have always been deeply committed to acquiring knowledge and understanding of economic theories, principles, and concepts.

____

____

____

- I have engaged in numerous aerospace engineering-related activities, which I found to be of great interest and fascination, and I was particularly enthralled by the intricate and cutting-edge nature of aerospace research and development.

- My involvement in various extracurricular activities during my undergraduate years has not only allowed me to gain valuable experiences but has also helped me to develop a well-rounded personality and improve my leadership and interpersonal skills, which I believe will be beneficial in my future academic pursuits.

8. Staunch Political Views

Academic institutions are committed to promoting diversity, inclusivity, and respect for different viewpoints; controversial political beliefs may come across as divisive or offensive to some members of the admission committee.

Examples:
- *Subscribing to the cause of death penalty abolition*
- *Supporting a particular political candidate or party*
- *Advocating for gun control or gun rights*
- *Taking a stance on abortion or reproductive rights*
- *Discussing the India-Pakistan or Ukraine-Russia conflict or other contentious geopolitical issues*

9. Redundancy

Buffalo buffalo Buffalo buffalo buffalo buffalo Buffalo buffalo. [xxix]

Perplexed? Not sure what these eight buffaloes are doing here?

Nonetheless, this is a grammatically correct sentence. However, repeating words, phrases, and expressions in your essay makes it unnecessarily verbose as well as diminishes the reader's interest. Hence, read your draft thoroughly to spot such *buffaloes* and purge them to make your text intelligible. Remember, your SOP has limited real estate, choose your words wisely and judiciously.

Example   1: *The   **final   outcome**   was **unexpected** and **surprising**.*

Edited   Sentence: *The   **outcome**   was **unexpected**.*

Example 2: *He personally met with **each** and **every** employee.*

Edited Sentence: *He personally met with **every** employee.*

Find and eliminate the redundancies in the sentences given below:

- The innovation is truly groundbreaking and revolutionary, as it introduces a completely novel and unique approach to solving common everyday problems, thereby offering a fresh and innovative solution that has never been seen or experienced before.

____

____

____

____

____

- The organization is currently in the process of conducting an extensive and comprehensive review of its operational procedures and practices, with the aim of identifying any potential areas where improvements and enhancements can be made to further optimize and improve its overall efficiency and effectiveness.

- She was overwhelmed with immense joy and happiness as she received the prestigious award for her exceptional and outstanding achievements in the field of scientific research and exploration.

- The luxurious mansion is situated in an exclusive and secluded location, providing its residents with a high degree of privacy and isolation from the outside world, allowing them to benefit from a serene and tranquil living environment.

- The seminar featured a panel of expert professionals who shared their valuable insights and experiences, offering a unique and one-of-a-kind opportunity for attendees to gain exclusive access to firsthand knowledge and information in the field of cutting-edge technological advancements.

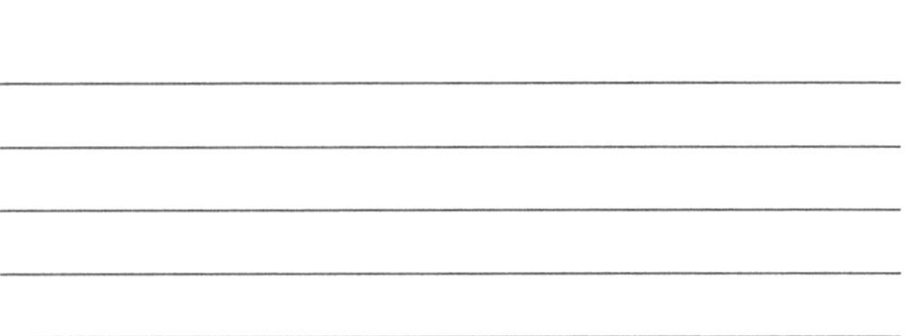

10. **Pretense**

Writing a statement of purpose that merely caters to the university's expectations rather than expressing genuine interests and goals can harm your chances of being admitted to the program.

"How can Admission Officers verify anything that we write in the essay?" asked one of my students. I replied, *"Wait until the interview call comes knocking."* And true to my words, he later reached out to express gratitude for instilling the value of *Honesty is the Best Policy*, as the interviewer was genuinely intrigued by his academic and personal achievements and wanted to know more about them.

Admission committees can easily spot insincere or inauthentic statements, and they may question our motivations for applying to their program. The SOP is your opportunity to showcase your unique perspective, passion, experience, and aspirations, and it is imperative to present yourselves honestly and confidently.

Following is a list of some *DON'Ts* straight from the university websites:

★ *Don't send out a boilerplate essay (Purdue* [xiii] *University)*

★ *Avoid using common cliches or generic quotes (University of Bath)* [xx]

★ *Don't write what you think we want to read. Write what you want to say! (Georgia Tech)* [viii]

★ *Using quotes or song lyrics may seem like a good starting point, but you are wasting valuable space with someone else's words (UIUC)* [xxiv]

★ *Avoid too many adjectives and adverbs; use short, direct sentences in an active voice. (Rice University)* [xiv]

★ *Don't write this (SOP) in one sitting (Arizona State University)* [i]

★ *Don't use slang or forced analogies (Harvard University)* [x]

★ *Don't make the mistake of sending a statement to XYZ school that says you really want to attend LMN school; that's an error that can strike you from being considered. (Virginia Tech)* [xxviii]

★ *Do not ask many people for feedback because it might become unfeasible to incorporate so many different suggestions in a single text. (Rice University)* [xiv]

★ *It is not necessary to sing the praises of the schools or the faculty. We are more interested in you and what you bring to the table. (Brown University)* [iii]

★ *Don't begin your essay with how you wanted to be a doctor at age 4 when you received your first Fisher Price doctor kit, the moment when you decided to be a doctor, or how heroes wear white coats. (Duke University)* [vii]

Please check the university websites you are applying to beforehand to ensure your SOP aligns with their specific requirements and instructions.

To summarize, steer clear of or eliminate the aforementioned mistakes while editing your essays to facilitate smooth run of your application process.

12

ADDRESSING THE WRITER'S BLOCK

Over the years, the most common and frequent complaints that I've received from students endeavoring to write their SOP include:

- I am unable to come up with new ideas!
- I am not sure how to proceed further!
- I am stuck!
- I am exhausted!
- I am on the nth version of my SOP but it's still not perfect! And so on...

This is called Writer's Block.

Writer's block is a condition where a writer experiences a creative slowdown or a complete lack of inspiration that makes it difficult to produce written work. It can be caused by various factors such as stress, anxiety, self-doubt, perfectionism, or even physical exhaustion.

Here are some ways to address writer's block:

1. **Pomodoro Technique**: Sometimes taking a break from writing can help clear your mind and allow you to return to your work with fresh eyes. In my experience, *Pomodoro technique*, developed by Francesco Cirillo, works the best to improve focus and productivity. Concentrate on your writing for 25 to 30 minutes, take a 5-minute break, recharge and rejuvenate, and get back to your writing with renewed enthusiasm.

   For how long have you been working on your SOP? When was the last time you took a break? Chart out your time management strategy below and make Cirillo proud.

____

____

____

____

____

____

____

____

____

____

---

2. **Change of environment**: Changing your environment, such as writing in a different location or taking a walk, can help stimulate your creativity.

   Suggest 5-6 places (inside and outside your house) where you can sit and work on your SOP peacefully, distraction-free.

---

3. **Brainstorm**: I have discussed brainstorming techniques in detail in Chapter 5 to help you overcome your writer's block and organize your thoughts better.

   What brainstorming activity suits you the most? And which one was your least favorite? Please provide two reasons to support your responses.

   ____

   ____

   ____

   ____

   ____

   ____

   ____

   ____

   ____

   ____

   ____

4. **Break the task into smaller pieces**: Breaking down the writing task into smaller, manageable pieces can help make it less overwhelming and more achievable.

Use the space below to create a flowchart of your writing process and visualize the steps involved.

____

____

____

____

____

____

____

____

____

____

____

____

5. **Seek support:** Talking to friends, family, or fellow writers can help provide encouragement and support. Share your write-ups with others and get their comments and feedback.

Do you have a teacher, a senior, or a sibling who can proofread your SOP? Prepare a quick list of your reviewers.

____

____

Overall, it is essential to recognize that although writer's block is a common phenomenon (I experienced it multiple times while authoring this paperback), it's absolutely possible to overcome it with perseverance, patience, and a willingness to try new ways.

13

READ TO WRITE

This chapter will highlight the symbiotic relationship between reading and writing. There is no specific age or time to start reading or foster a reading habit; rather, it should start from an early age. Interestingly, my journey with reading commenced in 6th grade, when I received my most treasured possession, *Pride and Prejudice* by Jane Austen, as a prize for winning a creative writing competition. It was an abridged version, but it opened my mind to a world of ideas, skills, and understanding. Since then, my love for reading has only grown stronger.

Drawing from my own experience, I strongly encourage everyone to engage in daily reading of fiction, non-fiction, articles, or newspapers as a way to enhance their writing skills. While there are countless benefits to reading, I want to highlight five key aspects that can help you cultivate a comprehensive approach to essay writing.

1. **Writing Style and Voice Development:** Reading various books will expose you to different authors' writing styles and voices. By observing and analyzing these styles, you can develop your own voice and writing style. Through experimentation inspired by different authors, you can find your preferred method of expression, making your essays more authentic and engaging.

   Write down the names of two books from the same genre but different authors and note what was unique about their writing styles.

   Example: *Agatha Christie and Lucy Foley. In my opinion, while both authors excel in the genre of mystery, Agatha Christie's style tends to focus on concise and plot-driven narratives, whereas Lucy Foley's writing leans toward atmospheric and character-driven storytelling.*

---

2. **Idea Generation and Critical Thinking:** Regular reading exposes you to a multitude of ideas, perspectives, and themes. This exposure will broaden your knowledge base, spark creativity, and enhance your analytical thinking skills. Engaging with different narratives will help you analyze, evaluate, and form opinions, which in turn strengthens your ability to generate original and well-informed ideas for your essays.

Share the names of a few books that have expanded your understanding of different ideas, cultures, and experiences while nurturing empathy and personal growth.

Example: *Thousand Splendid Suns by Khaled Hosseini, The Book Thief by Markus Zusak, 1984 by George Orwell, and Catch22 by Joseph Heller offer diverse perspectives, tackle pertinent social issues, and have encouraged me to think critically about the world around me.*

____

____

____

____

____

____

____

———————————————————————

———————————————————————

———————————————————————

3. **Structure and Organization:** By reading books from various genres, you will have examples of effective storytelling structures, character development, and plot progression. This exposure will help you understand how to organize your essays coherently. You can learn about introductions, transitions, paragraph development, and conclusions, enabling you to structure your own essays effectively and engage your readers.

> **Example**: *Classics such as To Kill A Mockingbird by Harper Lee, 1984 by George Orwell, and The Great Gatsby by F. Scott Fitzgerald introduced me to engaging introductions, well-structured paragraphs, effective transitions, and insightful or thought-provoking conclusions that reflected on the character's growth and journey.*

———————————————————————

———————————————————————

———————————————————————

———————————————————————

———————————————————————

———————————————————————

____

____

____

4. **Vocabulary Expansion:** A diverse range of books will expose you to various writing styles, genres, and vocabulary. This exposure will help you expand your vocabulary repertoire, enabling you to express your ideas more effectively in your essays. A broader vocabulary will allow you to choose precise and engaging language, making your writing impactful.

> **Example**: *I would highly recommend reading short stories by O' Henry, novels by Paulo Coelho, and autobiographies like The Becoming by Michelle Obama to expand your lexicon. Learn two new vocabulary words every day, along with their meaning and usage.*

Mention at least 5 books you read that required you to use dictionary.

____

____

____

____

____

____

____

____

5. **Empathy and Persuasive Writing:** Literature often explores complex human experiences, societal issues, and diverse perspectives. Reading books allows you to develop empathy and a more profound understanding of diverse cultures, backgrounds, and experiences. This empathy will enhance your ability to write persuasively as you learn to consider multiple viewpoints and craft compelling arguments supported by evidence and empathy.

> **Example**: *In addition to all the abovementioned genres and authors, I would like to add Newspaper Editorials. Editorials are opinion pieces written by experts, journalists, or influential figures who provide their perspective on various topics of public interest. By regularly engaging with newspaper editorials, you can develop a broader perspective, sharpen your logical reasoning skills, and gain insights into the diverse tapestry of human experiences and ideas.*

Share the latest news article that left a lasting impact on you and why.

____

____

____

____

____

To summarize, reading helps you to discover diverse writing styles, expands your vocabulary, improves grammar and syntax, sparks creativity, and enhances analytical and research skills. This practice not only elevates your language abilities and nurtures your distinct writing voice, but also sparks the birth of fresh ideas, empowers you to structure your essays with precision, and instills within you a genuine understanding of persuasive writing.

Here's a recommended reading list to help improve your writing skills and vocabulary:

Publications

- *The New York Times* or *The Economist*: Regularly reading articles from these publications will expose you to complex, high-level English.
- *The Wall Street Journal*: Another source of sophisticated business-related English.

Classic Literature

- *Pride and Prejudice* by Jane Austen
- *Moby-Dick* by Herman Melville

- *The Great Gatsby* by F. Scott Fitzgerald
- *To Kill a Mockingbird* by Harper Lee
- *1984* by George Orwell
- *Brave New World* by Aldous Huxley

Non-Fiction Books

- *The Selfish Gene* by Richard Dawkins
- *Outliers* by Malcolm Gladwell
- *Freakonomics* by Steven D. Levitt and Stephen J. Dubner
- *Atomic Habits* by James Clear
- *Sapiens* by Yuval Noah Harari

Essays and Short Stories

- Essays by Ralph Waldo Emerson and Henry David Thoreau
- *The Complete Short Stories* by Edgar Allan Poe
- *The Best American Essays* compilation, by various authors

Scientific Journals and Academic Papers

- Depending on the field you are interested in, reading articles from reputable journals such as *Scientific American* can help you get accustomed to technical language and complex ideas.

Vocabulary Building

- *Word Power Made Easy* by Norman Lewis: This book systematically helps build your vocabulary.

Grammar

- *Blue Book of Grammar and Punctuation* by Jane Straus and Lester Kaufman: This book is particularly useful for writers, students, and professionals who need to produce clear and error-free written communication.

- *High School English Grammar & Composition* by Wren & Martin: A useful tool for anyone looking to strengthen their English language skills, particularly in the context of the Indian educational system.

- *The Elements of Style* by William Strunk Jr.: Anyone looking to improve their writing skills can kickstart their journey with this book.

14

USING AI TOOLS FOR ESSAY WRITING

Some say, '*Work smarter, not harder.*' Being tech-savvy, I encourage the use of technology to reduce human efforts and save time for more productive work. However, when it comes to creative writing, I would beg to differ. Let me elaborate using some real examples.

I wanted to write an essay describing the day I came back home after two years of studying in the US. It was kept a surprise for my family except for my younger brother, who helped me execute this plan successfully. I tried entering (or explaining) the essay prompt to various AI tools and here is what I got:

RESPONSE 1 FROM AI TOOL

As the airplane touched down on familiar soil, I could not help but feel an electric surge of anticipation. It had been an entire year since I left for the United States to pursue my Master's degree, and now, in the quiet darkness of the night, the time had come to reunite with my family. Little did I know that my brother had conspired to turn this momentous occasion into an unforgettable surprise. With a mischievous glimmer in his eyes, he had slipped away from the house, leaving no trace of his intentions.

Feedback: Good attempt. I liked the use of vocabulary and sense words here, as it gives a professional touch to the essay. However, the context is still missing. I tried enhancing my inputs to get a better, more creative response.

RESPONSE 2 FROM AI TOOL

The pitch-black night sky hung above me like a velvet curtain as I stepped out of the airport, the fatigue of a long flight fading away in the presence of exhilaration. Little did my family know, a secret was brewing, a surprise in the making. As I navigated through the deserted arrivals terminal, my heart raced with anticipation. But just as uncertainty began to creep in, a familiar figure emerged from the shadows, adorned with a mischievous grin. It was my brother – the epitome of audacity and the guardian of my clandestine plan.

Feedback: The second response (it was probably the 4th or 5th attempt) shown above is different from the first one; however, it is full of purple prose, flowery language, and details that are not needed. Although sentence structure is coherent, it lacks emotions.

RESPONSE 3 FROM AI TOOL

"Everyone's fast asleep. I will leave in exactly four hours." whispered Sid in a soft, low, but anxious voice. He was doing this for the first time and that too well after the bewitching hour when you could hear crickets chirping and leaves rustling. Don't get him wrong. He was not going to meet his girlfriend. As a matter of fact, he was coming to receive me (his younger sister) at the airport. We had planned a surprise for our family, as I was coming back to India after two years of college studies in the US. And this was the first time I had used an inflight satellite phone to take stock of the situation at home.

Anyways, the craziest part of the plan was for my brother to get out of the house and get the car out of the garage without making the slightest sound in the dead of the night. Drop a pin and our entire plan could get foiled, as my grandmother was a light sleeper. And the first thought that would have come to her mind was, "Is that a burglar?"

Moreover, if my mom, a hard taskmaster, came to know that I was coming home without informing anyone in advance (a common etiquette followed by every Indian), she would admonish not only my brother and me but also my father (for reasons you cannot even think of).

Feedback: The third and the last response was generated by an AI (*Actual Intelligence*) tool commonly known as the *Human Brain*, which in this case belonged to me. Here, I have added dialogue and conversation to take the reader back in time to when this incident took place.

As seen from the above example, AI tools lack creativity and emotions. No matter how well-framed your question (or input) is, the output will lack *Personal Voice*. And it's this personal touch that makes your essay interesting and riveting to read.

AI tools can be used as a tool for inspiration, idea generation, or general guidance, but the responsibility of crafting a well-researched, coherent, and original essay ultimately lies with you – the writer.

15

ANALYZING SOP EXCERPTS

To reinforce the learnings from this book, I've included select passages from some very successful SOPs and offered my insights. Please review these excerpts and endeavor to spot unique qualities, characteristics, and narrative techniques to elevate your own SOP. Reiterating, please be advised that these excerpts are for demonstration purposes only and any form of replication is totally discouraged.

Excerpt 1:

"Sometimes you cannot be a hero.
Sometimes you must be a silent
guardian, a watchful protector."
~ The Dark Knight

Frontline workers embody this very spirit in our real world. They are the watchful protectors, tirelessly serving and safeguarding our communities, often without seeking recognition or glory. My aunt was one of these watchful protectors, a genuine hero who wholeheartedly devoted herself to the care of her patients, ultimately losing her life to the Covid-19 pandemic. Her work and life serve as a profound inspiration, motivating me to pursue a career as a Nurse and commit myself to serving both the nation and its people.

Feedback: Powerful introduction. The applicant has used dialogue from a movie to illustrate their awakening and support the real-life incident that impacted their life goals.

Excerpt 2:

After completing my MBA degree, my immediate goal is to work for a consulting firm such as Wells Fargo or Deloitte, enabling me to collaborate with diverse organizations across various industries. By working in these settings, I will gain valuable insights not only in finance but also in the overall management and operations of these organizations. This experience will serve as a stepping stone towards my long-term aspiration of joining my family's business of Travel and Hospitality Management.

My vision is to enhance and expand our chain of hotels on a global scale, diversifying them further.

Achieving this ambitious objective necessitates profound knowledge in management and finance, as well as hands-on experience in both domains. I firmly believe that pursuing an MBA from [University Name] will equip me with the necessary skills and expertise to accomplish my goals.

Feedback: The applicant has clearly defined short-term goal and how it will help them achieve their long-term goal of aggrandizing the family business.

Excerpt 3:

Upon completing my bachelor's degree in 2020, I embarked on my professional journey at Qualcomm Technologies, where I was privileged to be a part of their flagship "Snapdragon" project. As a Business Analyst, my role involved conducting in-depth statistical analysis on various aspects of the project, performing sanity checks, and engaging with clients to understand user preferences. Leveraging my academic expertise, I meticulously analyzed user data, user activity, and behavior, presenting detailed insights to higher management to aid in decision-making.

In 2022, I craved a closer understanding of business complexities, which motivated me to join Intel Corporation as a Business Intelligence Analyst. This move aligned perfectly with my aspirations, allowing me to gain exposure to pricing management, business planning and strategy formulation, and building Power BI dashboards of products for global stakeholders. Thus far, I have contributed to five advanced analytical projects, honing my business analysis skills through hands-on experiences in data engineering, machine learning, text analytics, data modeling, and visualization techniques. My dedication and innovative approach were recognized through awards and accolades like "Solvers for Tomorrow," "Pat on the Back," and so on; thereby fueling my passion for delving deeper into the realm of Business Analysis and expanding my skills and knowledge through a Master's degree.

Feedback: The applicant has provided a succinct description of the responsibilities and learnings from both jobs, along with a fitting rationale for transitioning jobs and for pursuing a graduate degree.

Excerpt 4:

To gain a deeper insight into the operations of the fashion industry, I completed two internships in 2018 and 2019, one at Modeling World in Mumbai and the other at Fashion Soiree in Bangalore. During these internships, I assimilated fundamental concepts related to visual merchandising, inventory management, and the retail environment. Additionally, I honed my ability to select ready-made outfits and accessories that aligned perfectly with clients' preferences, body language, and personal styles. My keen eye for the latest trends and creative styling techniques garnered praise and recognition from my supervisors.

Following these internships, I embarked on my graduation project at Panache Fashion Consultants in Gurgaon. Here, I not only styled supermodels and showstoppers but also took on the responsibility of sourcing exquisite jewelry, footwear, and accessories tailored to my client's measurements and requirements. This experience allowed me to collaborate with some of the top couturiers like Anita Dongre and Sabyasachi and avant-garde luxury stores like DLF and Le Mill that specialize in merchandise management in my country.

Through my cumulative experiences, I gained a profound understanding of the distinction between ready-to-wear and haute couture. Moreover, I enhanced my fashion sensibilities, business acumen, and leadership skills. This journey has fueled my desire to delve deeper into Fashion Styling and Management, motivating me to pursue a master's degree in this field.

Feedback: The applicant has eloquently demonstrated their passion for fashion and their learnings from real-world experiences. Moreover, applicant's focus and purpose of pursuing a Master's degree has enhanced the effectiveness of these paragraphs.

Excerpt 5:

My journey into the world of marine conservation has been marked by practical experiences that have solidified my commitment to this field. Through participation in the Coral Reef Health Assessment Project, the Micro-nano-plastic Analysis research publication, and community service at a public aquarium, I witnessed firsthand the intricate relationships within aquatic ecosystems and the role marine scientists play in understanding and preserving them. During my senior year of high school, excelling in biology, chemistry, and environmental science courses further fortified my passion for marine conservation, equipping me with the knowledge and skills to address the complex challenges faced by our oceans. As I embark on my undergraduate journey, I am eager to continue exploring the ocean's mysteries, contribute to conservation efforts, and make a meaningful impact in this field by pursuing marine conservation major.

Feedback: The applicant has concisely talked about their interest and career goals in Marine Conservation and supported the argument through examples of their project work, research paper, and curriculum. The applicant has not elaborated their roles and responsibilities because, for a 350-word undergraduate SOP, it's advisable to dedicate not more than 200 words to your academic and co-curricular experiences.

Excerpt 6:

After completing my BBA degree, I made a life-changing decision: instead of heading straight into a lucrative corporate job, I chose to venture into the heart of rural areas, where facilities are often scarce and communities struggle to access basic amenities like electricity and water. My motivation was simple but profound: I wanted to make a meaningful impact on the lives of children. Over the span of four years, I started makeshift classrooms in remote villages, under trees, and sometimes in the open air. I tailored a curriculum to their needs, fostering not only academic growth but also confidence and creativity.

The impact was astounding and heartwarming. Children who once struggled with basic skills now excelled academically and, more importantly, believed in their potential. This experience solidified my passion for social development. And I now aspire to pursue MBA in Non-profit Management from Booth School of Business, driven to continue advocating for the rights and opportunities of disadvantaged children through specialized knowledge and right direction.

Feedback: Well-structured narrative that effectively communicates applicant's journey, motivations, and aspirations. Applicant's contribution to marginalized community is inspiring and showcases their genuine commitment to making a positive impact on society.

Excerpt 7:

Throughout my school and college years, I have actively participated in various extracurricular activities, discovering invaluable lessons along the way. These pursuits, from excelling in Squash tournaments at district, state, and national levels to attaining Diploma in Kathak, an Indian Classical Dance form, have been more than just hobbies for me. I've not only gained valuable skills but also cultivated a deeper understanding of the importance of focus, physical fitness, and self-confidence in life. These activities have become the cornerstones of my personal growth and positive mindset, reminding me that life's most profound lessons are often learned outside of the four walls of the classroom.

Feedback: The essay offers insight into applicant's extracurricular activities and how their interest in sports and dance have influenced their personal growth. It is allowing the reader to better understand the applicant's personality and interests outside academics.

Excerpt 8:

In support of my academic aspirations, I have cultivated valuable skills in literature review and presentation through active participation in a diverse range of research conferences and seminars. Among these experiences, the acceptance of my paper titled "Carbon Credits: A World of

Possibilities" at the United Nations SDG Summit 2023 is worth a mention. Through my research, I endeavored to explain the role of Carbon credits in reducing greenhouse gas emissions - a major contributor to climate change. This paper is slated for publication in IEEE, underscoring its real-world significance.

My research has been underpinned by a sincere commitment to solving global warming through the application of technology. Consequently, it has further ignited my passion for pursuing advanced studies in Environmental Biology.

Feedback: The applicant appears to be highly driven with a strong commitment to their academic and research pursuits. The acceptance of their paper at the United Nations SDG Summit and IEEE suggests that their research is not only of high quality but also holds significant academic and possibly even real-world importance. Their focus on the topic of "Carbon Credits" indicates a keen interest in environmental issues and a desire to contribute to solving pressing global challenges.

Excerpt 9:

Given my zest for challenges and [University Name]'s mission of "nurturing changemakers," accomplishing my vision of establishing virtual, technologically-advanced primary schools in developing nations feels within reach. Expressing my utmost commitment to excellence, I genuinely hope [University Name] accepts my application and assists me in transforming the face of education system.

Feedback: The applicant has wrapped up the Statement of Purpose effectively by aligning their objectives with the University's vision statement.

BONUS CHAPTERS

16

VISA SOP

Writing SOP for a student visa application is an integral part of the process. This document helps immigration authorities understand your educational goals, objectives, and eligibility for the student visa.

For a Visa SOP, in addition to your academic SOP, you will be asked to:

- **Demonstrate your financial capacity** to cover tuition fees, living expenses, and any other costs associated with your studies overseas. Provide evidence of sufficient funds, such as bank statements or sponsorship letters, if required.

- **Explain your ties to your home country**, emphasizing your intention to return after completing your studies. This could include family, property, future employment prospects, or any other commitments.

- **Explain your reason for choosing this particular country** for pursuing higher education instead of your own. Emphasize the excellence of its education system, research opportunities, and overall infrastructure, without casting any negative light on your home country.

Before you start, thoroughly read, and understand the visa SOP requirements and guidelines provided by the consulate or embassy of the country you plan to study in. Each country may have specific requirements.

Sample student visa SOP paragraph for Canada

My decision to return to India after completing my Master's degree in Economics at the University of Toronto is rooted in a deep sense of responsibility and a strong desire to contribute to my country's development. India, as one of the world's fastest-growing economies, faces numerous complex challenges, including poverty alleviation, environmental sustainability, and healthcare reform. I believe that informed and evidence-based public policies are instrumental in addressing these issues effectively. I am particularly drawn to government organizations like the Ministry of Finance, NITI Aayog, and the Reserve Bank of India, which play pivotal roles in shaping India's economic landscape.

I understand the importance of abiding by Canadian immigration laws and regulations during my stay in Canada and am fully committed to maintaining a strong academic record. I have secured the necessary funds for my tuition and living expenses through a combination of personal savings, scholarships, and financial support from my family.

Sample student visa SOP paragraph for Germany

Returning to India after completing a graduate degree in Aeronautical Engineering from TU Munich, Germany, presents an exciting opportunity to contribute to the growth and development of my nation's aerospace and space exploration sectors. Opportunities at ISRO, PRL, and DRDO are not only professionally rewarding but will also help contribute to the nation's scientific and technological progress. Moreover, these roles will provide me a chance to work on exciting projects like Chandrayaan-4 while aligning my goals with the 'Make in India' campaign to bolster India's aerospace and defense capabilities.

Analyze the Australian Student Visa SOP prompt [ii] below and justify your reason for returning to your home country:

All applicants for a Student visa must show they are coming to Australia temporarily to gain a quality education. In the online student visa application form, you will need to provide a personal statement in English addressing the Genuine temporary entrant (GTE) requirement. This statement is to be 300 words in total (a 2000 character limit applies). The statement needs to address your personal circumstances for undertaking your proposed study in Australia. We encourage you to provide evidence or information about:

- *Previous study*
- *Gap in previous study*
- *Current employment*
- *Ties to home country or country of residence*
- *Economic situation in home country or country of residence*
- *Employment in a third country*
- *Situations in your home country (or country of residence)*
- *Potential situation in Australia*
- *Value of the course to your future*
- *Your immigration history*

____

____

____

____

____

____

____

Remember to start the visa application process well in advance to account for any processing times or delays.

17

SCHOLARSHIP SOP

Universities require a Scholarship Statement of Purpose before granting financial awards to students, primarily to assess the merit of applicants and determine their alignment with the scholarship's objectives. The SOP helps in evaluating candidates beyond academic achievements, offering a comprehensive view of their qualifications, personal aspirations, and potential impact. Ultimately, SOPs play a key role in helping universities select the most deserving candidates for scholarships while ensuring that the recipients are committed to their stated educational and career goals.

As a student, it falls upon you to instill confidence in the Financial Aid Committee regarding your abilities and future aspirations. A fundamental distinction between the Scholarship SOP and the Academic SOP lies in answering the question: *What makes you a deserving candidate for this award or grant?* To address this question, consider the following:

1. Have you been granted any scholarships or financial assistance during your academic journey?
2. Are you currently engaged in part-time or full-time employment to contribute to your family's financial well-being?
3. Will pursuing education abroad have a significant impact on your family's financial circumstances?
4. Are you a recipient of any outstanding recognition or do you possess some exemplary skills or experiences that set you apart from other applicants?
5. How will receiving this scholarship help you achieve your academic and career objectives?

Once you have answered these questions, writing a resounding Scholarship Essay becomes quite easy. Following is a sample paragraph for a Scholarship SOP:

During my undergraduate studies at LD Engineering College, I was the recipient of an academic excellence award of INR 80,000. Moreover, I secured a scholarship of USD 5000 from Project XYZ, for my ground-breaking 'Book Exchange App'. These awards are a testament to my sincere efforts; and I am proud to share that I could successfully fund my entire college education, independently. Now, as I embark on my educational journey at Dartmouth University, I am eager to continue this tradition of self-sufficiency by reducing the financial burden on my single-earner middle-class Indian Joint Family. The substantial tuition costs and living expenses in the United States, coupled with the unpredictable nature of the Indian Rupee, directly affect my family's annual budget. Financial aid from Dartmouth would not only expedite the repayment of my education loan but also grant me the precious gift of more dedicated study time, alleviating the need for on-campus jobs.

Below are few examples of actual Scholarship SOP Prompts for your reference.

★ **University of Illinois, Chicago Provost's Graduate Research Award:** [xxiii]

> *Plans for Future Funding and Justification of Financial Need (1 page).*
>
> *The applicant should report their current funding situation, provide a brief statement justifying financial need for the award, and lay out future plans for external funding during the duration of the thesis/dissertation/capstone project.*

★ **The University of Sydney, Sydney International Student Award:** [xviii]

> *In this personal statement, you will be asked to:*
>
> - *Tell us about yourself (maximum 200 words)*

- *Tell us what has inspired you to apply to the University (maximum 200 words)*
- *Tell us what you want to achieve with your studies at the University or how it will help you to achieve your goals (maximum 200 words)*

★ **San Jose State University (SJSU) Graduate Equity Fellowship:** [xv]

A personal statement with a clear, persuasive narrative highlighting your strengths and ability to perform at a high level of academic excellence. It informs reviewers of who you are and how you engage with and meet your academic, personal, and career goals. The personal statement is your opportunity to explain challenges you have faced and overcome; what motivates your interest in graduate study and determination to succeed in it; and the abilities, skills, and experience you possess that enhance your chances of success.

★ **University of Cambridge, Gates Cambridge Scholarship:** [xxii]

In not more than 500, words please explain why you are applying for a Gates Cambridge Scholarship and how you meet the four main criteria. Please describe how your interests and achievements, both academic and extra-curricular, demonstrate a capacity for leadership, commitment to using your knowledge to serve your community and to applying your talents to improve the lives of others.

★ **University of California, Berkeley, Berkeley Law Opportunity Scholarship (BLOS):** [xxi]

You are required to submit a one to two page essay addressing the following prompt: How do you think being a first generation college student has shaped your perspective, and how will that perspective contribute to the Berkeley Law community and the broader legal profession?

For universities which do not require any additional scholarship essay or application, you may consider incorporating a line or two in the academic SOP requesting financial aid.

Example: *An assistantship or scholarship would play a significant role in making my dream of attending your esteemed institution a reality, as financial constraints would otherwise confine it to mere wishful thinking.*

Please be aware that seeking a need-based scholarship could potentially impact your prospects of admission. Therefore, pursue this avenue only if paying tuition is a genuine challenge for you and your family.

THINK OUT LOUD

THINK OUT LOUD

REFERENCES

i.   Arizona State University. (n.d.). *Personal Statement | Admission.* Retrieved October 19, 2023, from https://admission.asu.edu/graduate/personal-statement

ii.   Australian Government - Department of Home Affairs. (2022, October 6). *Genuine Temporary Entrant Requirement.* Retrieved from https://immi.homeaffairs.gov.au/visas/getting-a-visa/visa-listing/student-500/genuine-temporary-entrant

iii.   Brown University - Brown-RISD Master of Arts in Design Engineering. (n.d.). *Apply | Design Engineering.* Retrieved October 20, 2023, from https://design.engineering.brown.edu/sites/default/files/MADE%20Personal%20Statement%20Guidelines%202022.pdf

iv.   California Institute of Technology - Graduate Studies Office. (n.d.). *Application Requirements.* Retrieved September 9, 2023, from https://www.gradoffice.caltech.edu/documents/6314/supplemental_documents.pdf

v.   Cornell University - The Learning Strategies Center. (n.d.). *The Cornell Note Taking System.* Retrieved October 31, 2023, from https://lsc.cornell.edu/how-to-study/taking-notes/cornell-note-taking-system/

vi.   Delft University of Technology. (n.d.). *Non-Dutch BSc Degree.* Retrieved September 9, 2023, from https://www.tudelft.nl/en/education/programmes/masters/engineering-and-policy-analysis/msc-engineering-and-policy-analysis/application-and-admission/non-dutch-bsc-degree

vii.   Duke University. (n.d.). *Personal Essay | Advising.* Retrieved October 20, 2023, from https://advising.duke.edu/prehealth/apply/personal-essay/

References

viii.   Georgia Institute of Technology. (n.d.). *Personal Essays | Undergraduate Admission*. Retrieved October 19, 2023, from https://admission.gatech.edu/first-year/personal-essays

ix.   Harvard University - Harvard Graduate School of Education. (n.d.). *Ed.M. and Ed.L.D. Application Requirements*. Retrieved September 9, 2023, from https://www.gse.harvard.edu/sites/default/files/2023-09/Statement-of-Purpose.pdf

x.   Harvard University | Mignone Center for Career Success. (n.d.). *Applying to Medical School*. Retrieved October 19, 2023, from https://careerservices.fas.harvard.edu/applying-to-medical-school/

xi.   Johns Hopkins University - Bloomberg School of Public Health. (n.d.). *How to Apply*. Retrieved October 17, 2023, from https://publichealth.jhu.edu/offices-and-services/office-of-admissions-services/how-to-apply

xii.   Max-Planck-Gesellschaft - Max Planck Institute of Immunobiology And Epigenetics. (n.d.). *Application procedure*. Retrieved September 9, 2023, from https://www.ie-freiburg.mpg.de/2053634/Application_Hints

xiii.   Purdue University - Purdue OWL. (n.d.). *Statements of Purpose: Drafting Your Statement*. Retrieved October 19, 2023, from https://owl.purdue.edu/owl/general_writing/graduate_school_applications/graduate_school_applications_statements_of_purpose/statements_of_purpose_drafting_your_statement.html

xiv.   Rice University - Graduate and Postdoctoral Studies . (n.d.). *Writing a killer Statement of Purpose* . Retrieved October 20, 2023, from https://graduate.rice.edu/news/current-news/writing-killer-statement-purpose

xv.   San José State University - College of Graduate Studies. (2021, May 24). *Tips for a Successful Application*. Retrieved from https://www.sjsu.edu/cgs/financial-support/graduate-equity-fellowship/tips-application.php

References

xvi.   Stanford University - Graduate School of Education. (n.d.). *Application Requirement for PhD, MA, MS*. Retrieved October 10, 2023, from https://ed.stanford.edu/admissions/application-reqs/programs

xvii.   The University of Chicago. (n.d.). *Application Requirements | Master of Arts Program in the Social Sciences*. Retrieved September 9, 2023, from https://mapss.uchicago.edu/apply/application-requirements

xviii.   The University of Sydney. (n.d.). *Sydney International Student Award*. Retrieved October 20, 2023, from https://www.sydney.edu.au/study/fees-and-loans/scholarships/sydney-international-student-award.html

xix.   UCLA - Anderson School of Management. (n.d.). *Requirements*. Retrieved September 9, 2023, from https://www.anderson.ucla.edu/degrees/full-time-mba/admissions/requirements

xx.   University of Bath. (n.d.). *Writing a personal statement for an undergraduate course*. Retrieved October 19, 2023, from https://www.bath.ac.uk/guides/writing-a-personal-statement-for-an-undergraduate-course/

xxi.   University of California, Berkeley - Berkeley Law. (n.d.). *Berkeley Law Opportunity Scholarship*. Retrieved October 7, 2023, from https://www.law.berkeley.edu/admissions/jd/financial-aid/types-of-aid/scholarships/entering-student-scholarships/berkeley-law-opportunity-scholarship/

xxii.   University of Cambridge - Gates Cambridge Trust. (n.d.). *How to Apply for a Cambridge Scholarship*. Retrieved October 7, 2023, from https://www.gatescambridge.org/apply/how-to-apply/

xxiii.   University of Illinois Chicago - Graduate College. (n.d.). *Provost's Graduate Research Award*. Retrieved September 9, 2023, from https://grad.uic.edu/funding-awards/graduate-college-fellowships/pgra/

References

xxiv. University of Illinois Urbana-Champaign - The Career Center. (n.d.). *How to Write a Personal Statement*. Retrieved October 19, 2023, from https://www.careercenter.illinois.edu/howtopersonalstatement

xxv. University of Michigan Ann Arbor - College of Engineering - Department of Aerospace Engineering. (n.d.). *Application Process for Graduate Programs*. Retrieved September 9, 2023, from https://aero.engin.umich.edu/graduate/application-process/

xxvi. University of Oxford. (2023, September 22). *MSc in Public Policy Research*. Retrieved from https://www.ox.ac.uk/admissions/graduate/courses/msc-public-policy-research#content-tab--7

xxvii. University of Washington, Seattle - Paul G. Allen School of Computer Science & Engineering. (n.d.). *B.S./M.S. Application Information*. Retrieved September 9, 2023, from https://www.cs.washington.edu/academics/bsms/application

xxviii. Virginia Tech. (n.d.). *Writing personal statements | Career and Professional Development*. Retrieved October 20, 2023, from https://career.vt.edu/grad-school/writing-personal-statements.html

xxix. Wikipedia contributors. (2023, August 28). Buffalo buffalo Buffalo buffalo buffalo buffalo Buffalo buffalo. Wikipedia, The Free Encyclopedia. Retrieved October 11, 2023, from https://en.wikipedia.org/w/index.php?title=Buffalo_buffalo_Buffalo_buffalo_buffalo_buffalo_Buffalo_buffalo&oldid=1172589091

ABOUT THE AUTHOR

Nimisha Padliya is a certified Global Career Counsellor and an expert in the field of overseas education application process. With a profound passion for helping students achieve their academic dreams, she brings her extensive knowledge and personal  experiences to her first book, *How to Write an Admission Winning SOP.*

Nimisha finished her Bachelor's in Instrumentation & Control from L.D. College of Engineering, Gujarat University, India, and Master's in Electrical & Computer Engineering from North Carolina State University (NCSU), Raleigh, US. Her academic journey at NCSU and experience in the US as a whole, not only advanced her technical expertise but also inspired her to explore the world of education consultancy.

For the past decade, Nimisha has dedicated herself to the overseas education sector, where she has assisted aspiring students in crafting University applications. Her deep understanding of the admissions process, coupled with her genuine commitment to each student's success, has earned her a reputation as a trusted advisor in the field. Currently, she is working as a Lead Counsellor at Scholarly.

With her book, *How to Write an Admission Winning SOP*, Nimisha aims to share her wealth of knowledge and experience with aspirants worldwide. Through this book, Nimisha's dedication to making academic dreams a reality shines brightly, and her readers will find a credible guide in their pursuit of higher education.

9 798889 186476 4